To Gran

COMING

OUT

of the

BLACK

COUNTRY

—

Stanley
Underhill

Stanley Underhill

Copyright © Stanley R. Underhill, 2018
All rights reserved

The rights of Stanley R. Underhill to be identified as
the author of this work have been asserted in accor-
dance with Section 77 of the Copyright, Designs and
Patents Act 1988

Published by BCPress in 2021
www.comingoutoftheblackcountry.com

Cover: Photo and Design by Thomas Völker

A CIP record for this book
is available from the British Library
ISBN 978-1-5272-9662-6

First published in 2018 by Zuleika,
89G Lexham Gardens, London, W8 6JN

Designed by Euan Monaghan
Printed in England

A CIP record for this book
is available from the British Library
ISBN 978-1-9996232-1-0

This book is dedicated to all those who have been hurt or suffered persecution because of homophobia, and to those who have helped to bring awareness and acceptance of homosexuality to communities, Church and State. I hope that readers facing similar problems in their lives, many of which are still with us today, will find my story helpful. You are not alone.

Contents

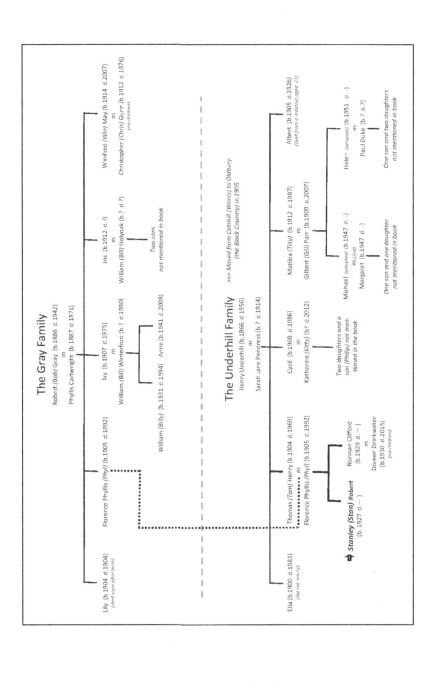

The Gray Family

Robert (Bob) Gray (b 1886 d.1942)
m
Phyllis Cartwright (b.1887 d 1971)

Lily (b.1904 d 1904)
(Died soon after birth)

Florence Phyllis (Phyl) (b.1905 d.1992)

Ivy (b.1907 d 1975)
m
William (Bill) Winterford (b.? d.1990)

Iris (b.1912 d.?)
m
William (Bill) Holyoak (b.? d.?)

Two sons
not mentioned in book

Winifred (Win) May (b.1914 d.2007)
m
Christopher (Chris) Gurn (b.1912 d.1976)
(no children)

William (Billy) (b.1931 d.1994)   Anne (b.1941 d.2008)

The Underhill Family

Henry Underhill (b.1866 d.1956)
m
Sarah Jane Pengress (b.? c.1914)

>>> Moved from Catshill (Worcs) to Oldbury
(the Black Country) in 1905

Ella (b.1900 d.1983)
(did not marry)

Thomas (Tom) Henry (b.1904 d.1969)
m
Florence Phyllis (Phyl) (b.1905 d.1992)

Cyril (b.1908 d.1986)
m
Katherine (Kitty) (b? d.2012)

Two daughters and a
son (Philip) not men-
tioned in the book

Matilda (Tilly) (b.1912 c.1987)
m
Gilbert (Gill) Parr (b.1909 c.2007)

Albert (b.1905 d.1926)
(Died from a mastoid aged 21)

↟ Stanley (Stan) Robert
(b.1927 d.—)
Norman Clifford
(b.1929 d.—)
m
Doreen Drinkwater
(b.1930 d.2015)
(no children)

Michael (adopted) (b.1947 d.—)
m (1st)
Margaret (b.1947 d.—)

One son and one daughter
not mentioned in book

Helen (adopted) (b.1951 d.—)
m
Paul Duke (b.? c.?)

One son and two daughters
not mentioned in book

Acknowledgements

I am greatly indebted to the Brothers of Charterhouse and friends for their constant encouragement and for their assistance in proofreading my book: Philip Bacon, Walter Balmford, The Rev. Canon Howard Cocks, John Davey, Mansel David, Charles Duff, Richard Franklin, Gerald Glover, Dudley Green, Patricia Hobson, Tom Hobson, The Rev. Robin Isherwood, The Rev. Dr Malcolm Johnson, Ann Kenrick, Father Brooke Kingsmill-Lunn, Simon Kitching, Mike Lawlor, Father Clive Lee, Rory Macpherson, Stephen McGhee, Father Richard Miller, Charles Neal, Jean Reed, The Rev. John Robson, Caroline Sherlock, Harry Sherman, the late Alan Scrivener, Terry Tastard, The Rev. Canon Colin Tolworthy, Liam West and The Rev. Peter Watkins.

I am very grateful to David Allison who gave many hours of his professional expertise in correcting, editing and suggesting improvements to my text and bringing my book to a stage where it was more acceptable for publishing. I am also indebted to Michael Young for proofreading and to Thomas Völker for designing the paperback edition. My friend Richard Norman has been an enormous help to me whilst writing this book, especially in selecting and enhancing the digital pictures for inclusion in the first edition. I am especially grateful to Jayne Ozanne for the very moving Foreword she wrote despite the many pressures on her time and to Norman Underhill, my brother, for his invaluable help in recollecting more accurately our experiences shared as children and teenagers before I fled the nest to join the Royal Navy.

Lastly, I would like to thank Tom Perrin of Zuleika for his enthusiasm and the kindness he has shown me in first publishing my book.

I have quoted from works still protected by copyright, but in each case, I have given details of the author and source of the quotation which have been incorporated in the text. Many of the people referred to in the book have been given another name despite the fact that most of them are no longer alive. Finally, I have included a bibliography of the books which have helped me over the years, especially other autobiographies of people who have faced similar problems, and books which have taught me how to interpret and understand the Bible.

Foreword

Stanley's letter was, quite literally, a God-send (See Appendix). Coming out of the blue on the eve of my Private Member's Motion debate at the General Synod of the Church of England to condemn Conversion Therapy, I very nearly didn't open it. The crisp white envelope with my name beautifully handwritten on front had to be – I assumed – yet another harsh letter telling me how wrong I was in seeking to protect some of God's most vulnerable children from the cruelty meted out by those in the Church.

I went to the Synod bar, ordered a drink and took a deep breath before reading it. Within minutes I was in tears. It was heart-breaking and inspiring in equal measure.

Here was a devout man of God, a true father of the Faith, who had personally experienced the full horror of a range of 'conversion therapy' techniques devised by both Church and State in order to ensure he might 'conform' to the norms expected of him. After a brief synopsis of the various procedures he had been through – which he details in depth in this moving memoir – it ended with a plea to Synod that the motion be passed.

I vowed that, somehow, I would find a way of sharing it with those gathered.

The debate of July 8th, 2017 was intense. It can be read in the 'Report on Proceedings' available on the Church of England website, or watched on YouTube. Towards the end of the two hours I realised that it would be impossible to respond in any meaningful way to all the speeches that had been made, so instead I decided to summarise Stanley's letter and heartfelt plea.

'I hope with all my heart that your Private Member's Motion asking the Synod that such treatment is unethical and harmful as it does not work, will now be accepted. May God support you in all your endeavours to bring about an end once and for all to the Church's homophobia in all its forms, which have throughout the ages caused so much misery and suffering to countless thousands of people who were made in the image of God.'

I went on to urge the Synod, for the sake of all those who like Stanley had suffered so much, to pass the motion. It did so, unanimously, in all three Houses of the Synod.

This book shares Stanley's journey. It is as heart-breaking and as inspiring as the letter he sent to me. It is a testimony to a man whose love of God and for his neighbour shines through, despite the darkness that constantly sought to engulf him, the cruelty he had to endure, and the loneliness which he had to contend with almost daily. It is a miracle that Stanley has survived – but survived he has against all odds and is, I know, one of the most radiant, kind and gentlest of men that I have ever had the privilege of knowing. For the sake of Stanley, and for the untold thousands who he rightly names and have lives that mirror his own, we must renew our resolve to work together for a more loving and accepting Church. One that preaches a Gospel that assures us that we are each made in the image of God, that we are loved with a passion by our Creator, and that the desire for love that is embedded in most of our hearts is a God-given desire that must be celebrated and embraced.

Jayne Ozanne
Director, Ozanne Foundation
May 2018

Preface

In January 1948 I completed National Service, was de-mobbed and began a career path as an accountant. I should have been on top of the world. Instead I found myself in a dingy church room, awaiting an exorcism. Afterwards would come a mental breakdown and recovery and a life-time of learning to love what I had been taught to despise: namely, my homosexuality.

The idea of writing an account of my struggle with my sexual orientation and subsequent depression was suggested to me by Charles Neal, a therapist and author whom I used to consult now and again to ease my pain. He thought that it could be cathartic. I resisted the idea for a long time as it seemed to me a somewhat self-indulgent exercise, but, on further reflection, I realised that my story might be of help and support to other people in a similar predicament. I also recognised that it would be more helpful to give the underlying and often complex issues involved flesh on the bare bones by incorporating them into a fuller autobiography of my long life. This is what I have endeavoured to do in the following pages.

My struggle with depression began in earnest when I was twenty-nine years old, after a mental breakdown brought about by my inability to accept my homosexuality. The depression has returned at intervals throughout my life – I am now ninety-one as I complete these reminiscences.

The medical profession is still not sure what exactly causes depression; some think that it is triggered by bad experiences in childhood. This was certainly true in my case. When I was a boy I was bullied at school, which caused me a lot of anxiety and unhappiness. The situation was compounded by my father's rejection of me because I did not fulfil his expectations of what he thought a boy should be.

During my teens and twenties, I wrestled with my homosexuality in a world which was ignorant and hostile about such matters. My state of mind throughout this period was defined by intense anxiety, confusion and a lack of confidence in myself – inner turmoil that ultimately resulted in a breakdown, precipitated by an exorcism by a Fundamentalist Christian who failed to deliver me from 'the demon', as he called it. At my request, I became a voluntary patient at the former Radcliffe-on-Trent mental hospital where I received electroconvulsive therapy (ECT). This undoubtedly dampened my anxiety but at the price of some loss of memory.

After my convalescence I returned to accountancy, but the anxiety over my sexuality continued to rage and gave way to the periodic depressions which have punctuated my life ever since. Usually triggered by stress caused by events in my life, these depressions were characterised by loss of motivation and a feeling of lethargy and ennui, followed by times of hyperactivity. Churchill referred to his depression as 'the black dog', and I cannot think of a better way to describe my descent into despondency and futility. After my retirement in 1994 from a Chaplaincy on the island of

Menorca, the periods of depression continued but were less frequent and not as deep as I had hitherto experienced. In my thirties I sought a variety of cures for my homosexuality. I was given, by the doctors at the mental hospital, a prescription for injections of the male hormone testosterone and underwent a course of Freudian psychoanalysis. For a while I took antidepressants but they had awful side effects, so I gave them up along with my quest for a cure. My only relief was to talk to a counsellor, therapist or spiritual director. Since Freud new models of counselling have evolved based on total respect and regard for the patient, thus establishing a relationship of acceptance, compassion and empathy between the patient and the counsellor. Unfortunately, I missed out on these more enlightened therapies.

What has astonished me in recalling these traumatic events, bearing in mind that some of them occurred over eighty years ago, is the feeling that they happened yesterday. I understand the reason for this is that the amygdala, a mass of nuclei located deep between the temporal lobes of the brain, automatically stores emotions like fear and anger. Even though the events happened decades ago, painful emotions felt at the time re-emerge as though they are happening now. However, it is also a known fact that we do not remember all the details of our childhood and that the brain unconsciously 'fills in' specific details. In other words, it recreates the memory. Many of the problems and difficulties with which I battled are still with us today. Fortunately, the advent of many organisations tackling such evils as homophobia, bullying and intolerance has gone hand-in-hand with better sex education, improved parenting and a deeper understanding of people who are suicidal. All have undoubtedly resulted in a kinder and more forgiving world.

* * *

My story is both autobiographical and chronological. Sometimes, however, it has been necessary to depart from the strict sequence of events, especially when sketching profiles of members of my family who have influenced my life. Inevitably, the story is about life in the valleys and on the plains – and occasionally on the mountain tops – but behind the scenes there is always the daily challenge of coping with my homosexuality and depression.

I have shared with readers what it was like growing up in the industrial part of the Black Country, going to a state school in the 1930s, and leaving on my fourteenth birthday to earn my living in the printing trade while WWII was raging. Just after the war ended, I was conscripted into the Royal Navy as a Sick Berth Attendant (SBA). Two years later I was demobilised and trained in Nottinghamshire for the accountancy profession, before practising as an accountant in London. In midlife, I left accountancy to join a religious order, after which I trained for the Anglican priesthood. Finally, I became a parish priest, serving both in England and abroad.

For most of my life I have been a committed Christian, having experienced a kind of Protestant conversion in my early twenties whilst a member of the Methodist

Church. However, as I became aware of my emerging homosexuality, I found it increasingly difficult to reconcile my sexuality with my Christian faith and with Christians who maintain that homosexuality is sinful and an abomination to God. My struggle with Fundamentalist Christianity compounded my difficulties, and it has taken many years to resolve the issue which has blighted the lives of so many people throughout history. It was heartening to hear Justin Welby, the Archbishop of Canterbury, at the meeting of the Anglican Bishops in September 2014 apologise for the hurt and pain the Anglican Church has inflicted on lesbian, gay, and transgender people. I never married and for the last thirty-six years I have been an ordained priest in the Church of England. I am most happy where I find a liberal Catholic theology, a compassionate community, and dignified sacramental liturgy.

Despite the struggles and challenges which have dominated my life and caused me much anger, frustration and unhappiness, I have tried to tell my story as objectively as possible - with honesty, integrity and charity. As the following pages will confirm, I was not born with a silver spoon in my mouth – a chip on the shoulder would be more accurate! Casting my mind back to nearly one hundred years ago has not been an easy experience, but as this book is the story of my life, I must begin at the beginning.

Chapter 1

THE WORLD I ENTERED

I come from an area in the middle of England known as the Black Country, which then covered a part of south Staffordshire, the northern tip of Worcestershire and part of Warwickshire. It is now called the West Midlands.

I entered this world in my maternal grandfather's house on the 4th April 1927 at 93, Barker Street, Rood End, Oldbury, where my mother had lived with her parents and three sisters.

My grandfather, Robert Gray, rented a substandard terraced house built in the late nineteenth century to house workers and their families flocking from the countryside for work. The street was slap-bang in the middle of a vast industrial sprawl where my grandfather worked in a factory as a die sinker, who made moulds and jigs to shape metal for parts of machinery. Next to it was the Langley Forge where my grandfather's brother, my mother's Uncle Ernie, worked on the furnaces at the side of a canal. As the house where I was born was too small to accommodate the new Underhill family, we were obliged to move to my father's parents' house a few doors away from Grandfather Gray. This house was also small, dark and cold, with primitive washing and sanitary facilities. Grandfather Underhill could not read and could barely write his name. He lost his wife when he was quite young and so had raised his two daughters and three sons on his own. How they all managed with only two bedrooms I do not know. 'Battery farming', a term that became current later in the century, would more accurately describe the way we all lived 'cheek by jowl'. We were squeezed into a tiny front room where we lived, ate, slept and did everything else.

When I was about six, I had to stay with Grandfather Underhill because my mother had to go into hospital and my father was unable to look after me. I had to share grandfather's bed, an experience never to be forgotten. Grandfather was as broad as he was high, so when he got into bed the other side of the mattress tilted up so violently that I had to cling to the side of the mattress to stop myself from rolling down the bed and into my grandfather, where I was in danger of being crushed!

Within spitting distance of my grandparents' houses were factories galore. There was Albright & Wilson, who manufactured the phosphorus bombs for the war, as well as toothpaste and custard powder. Oldbury Carriage Works made most of the tanks used in WWI. Accles & Pollocks made nuts and bolts. British Industrial Plastics made polyethylene used in radar, and Imperial Chemicals Company (ICI) made amongst other things: paint, acrylic, plastics and perspex. From Grandfather Underhill's house we could see their chimney stacks and taste the acrid, evil-smelling smoke which spewed out from them.

The smoke was so noxious that it would rot your curtains and spoil the washing on your line if the wind changed. In those days you could buy a special yellow dye which would prevent the curtains from rotting! When it rained the muck in the air would distil and coat the exterior of the houses and factories so that everywhere looked dirty and black. Hooters calling people to work filled the early morning air and resounded again in the evening when it was time to 'knock off'. Day and night the furnaces shot flames into the sky and the thud of hammers pounding the metal set a relentless beat. No wonder that Queen Victoria, on her second visit to Dudley Castle on 13th November 1866, ordered the carriage curtains to be drawn to block out the inferno. Every time I hear the line 'those dark satanic mills' from William Blake's poem *Jerusalem*, I am reminded of the place of my nativity. In 1882, Elihu Burritt, the American Consul in Birmingham, described the region as 'black by day and red by night'. It is said that J. R. R. Tolkien, who was brought up in Birmingham not far away, based the grim region of Mordor on the heavily industrialised Black Country in his famous novel *Lord of the Rings*. I suppose it was not until I was about twelve and had bought my twelve and sixpenny bike that I began to discover that England also had beautiful countryside, pastures and green hills outside the confines of this conglomeration of industrial works and factories which polluted the air and poisoned the earth.

Despite the contributions all these industries made to world trade and supplying the needs of two World Wars, little or none of the wealth created trickled down to the ordinary people. When I was a young man, I remember reading an article in the *Manchester Guardian* which reported that not a single mine owner, factory boss or local councillor lived within the Borough of Oldbury, as it was then; instead, they all had their abodes in the lush Worcestershire countryside. Even today, Sandwell is the third most deprived authority in the West Midlands after Birmingham and Stoke-on-Trent, and the fourteenth most deprived area in the UK.

Working conditions at the time were extremely hard. Tensions reached crisis point on 13th May 1926, when the General Council of the Trade Union Congress called a General Strike in an unsuccessful attempt to force the British government to prevent wage reductions and worsening conditions for 800,000 locked-out coal miners. Some 1.7 million workers downed tools, especially those in the transport and heavy industries, and although the strike only lasted ten days it remained in the consciousness of the ordinary people for a long time afterwards.

There are no recorded figures for Oldbury and the neighbouring towns, but in Wolverhampton six miles away 35,000 workers took part in the strike, shutting down the building trade, the car industry, and the buses and trams of the public transport system. When the strike ended, the miners who were re-employed were forced to accept even longer hours and lower wages while the rest had no choice but to go on the dole. The General Strike of 1926 followed by the Wall Street Crash of the New York Stock Exchange in 1929 ushered in the Great Depression, which spread to most of the industrialised countries of the world. Their economies did not begin to recover until the outbreak of the Second World War.

Witnessing the strike first-hand, my parents and relatives spoke of it often in bitter tones. My father, who worked for a time at Lucas Electrical Industries, referred to the wealthy owners of the factories and mines as 'skinflints'. At the very mention of William Morris – who became Lord Nuffield, the greatest industrialist of the age – he would fume about the poor pay and conditions of the workers in car factories built on the American model of mass production. Nor was father impressed by the great Lord's philanthropy when he founded Nuffield College at Oxford: he thought that the money should have been used to pay workers decent wages.

The demands of making a living and keeping your head above water meant that there was little time and energy left over for self-improvement, recreational or cultural pursuits. Poorly educated and unable to help ourselves, we lived in a culture of disappointment and gloom relieved only by escapist films and popcorn musicals from Hollywood. We were too poor to buy newspapers, only reading those occasionally passed on to us by relatives, and we were without a radio for long periods; consequently, we were largely ignorant of the rise of Communism, the Nazi Party in Germany, and the Spanish Civil War. We knew, however, about the British Union of Fascists because Oswald Mosley was the Labour MP for Smethwick, the neighbouring borough to Oldbury. Successive governments seemed at a loss as to how to relieve the suffering and distress of the people. It was only after WWII when the Labour Party brought in its unprecedented welfare reforms with their

National Health Service Act 1946 that life for ordinary people began to improve and confidence was restored.

This, then, was the world in which I grew up. Whatever has happened in my life, the Black Country inevitably has always been part of me and I have always been part of it.

Chapter 2

OUR SON IS NOT NORMAL

Many gay men attest to the fact that their parents found it hard to accept that they were 'different'. While writing this chapter I happened to see *The Making of Me*, the BBC documentary about John Barrowman, a talented actor, singer, and presenter. In it, Barrowman maintains that he was born gay and that it was not a personal lifestyle or choice. He also showed the Barbie dolls that he collected as a child. Although his parents were shocked, they accepted him and loved him for whom he was, and so he led a happy and healthy childhood. The following episode, one of my earliest recollections, will demonstrate just how different my childhood was.

I was about six when my Aunt Ella, my father's eldest sister who never married, took me shopping with her one day. I would not leave the shop until she had bought me a doll.

I remember quite clearly that it was a black doll, dressed in brightly coloured clothes, and it came in a toy wicker pram. When I came home pushing this pram with the doll in it, my father looked at me with utter disbelief. Even now, I can hear him calling to my mother, 'Phil, just yaw come 'ere and look at what 'e's got now!' Father was a man of few words and not good at articulating what he felt, but on this occasion his credulity was stretched to the limit. He just could not cope with this girly behaviour from his son.

The doll and pram episode occurred around the same time as the local authorities installed a bath in one of the bedrooms of our council house. From then on, my Aunty Ella came to our house every Friday night to take a bath. It was wonderful to have such a thing instead of being dunked in the kitchen sink. Years later my younger brother Norman told me that he was terrified of being lifted into the kitchen sink, a large earthenware receptacle which served many purposes. Sometimes I used to call for Kenny, the boy who lived next door to go to school with him and I saw that they had had their bath installed in the living room instead of the small bedroom and to my amazement they used it as a coal bunker! The stench of the house was bad enough, without adding the smell of the coal house to it! Thereafter I used to wait outside his house for Kenny. I often wondered about the Blundell's rationale about the location of the bath. Perhaps they were unwilling to give up the third bedroom as they already had four children?

Soon after our bath arrived, I caught the measles and was confined to the bedroom that I shared with my brother. My mother lit a fire in the small grate to make me more comfortable. It was winter, and the house was freezing cold – most of the windows had frosted up both inside and outside and my brother and I used to draw patterns on them, much to our mother's annoyance. The only room in which we had a regular fire, and consequently where we spent most of our time, was the kitchen. We could not afford the coal to heat the front

8

room except on special occasions, and the bedrooms were like ice boxes. One day mother left me to my own devices, and I stripped the doll of her clothes and burnt them in the fire. I then threw both the doll and the pram, together with the coal from the coal scuttle and the ornaments from the dressing table, out of the bedroom window onto the roof of the bay window beneath. Finally, I moved the bed right up against the fireplace. At that moment, my mother burst into the room and screamed, 'What on earth do yaw think yaw are doin', trying to burn the 'ouse down?' Make no mistake, I got a slap around the ears like I'd never had before. I'm still puzzled by my bizarre behaviour because I was not a destructive child. It might have been something to do with my fever or the boredom of being cooped up alone in the bedroom all day long. But I suspect getting rid of the doll was also a symbolic action: a protest at my father's increasing alienation from me, which only became more apparent as I got older.

* * *

My mother was fortunate in having a fine complexion, which she retained all her life. Beyond a dab of Pond's Cream or in later life a dab of Ulay, she never used make-up. Indeed, she often quoted a bit of doggerel, attributed to a Black Country lady named Winnie Watson, as a bit of propaganda against the use of make-up. It went like this:

Little dabs of powder,
Little dabs of paint,

Make a girl's complexion,
Look like what it ain't.

No wonder my mother took such exception when she
discovered that I had a make-up kit containing lipstick,
powder and so forth. At the time I was friendly with Te-
resa, the daughter of one of our neighbours. Everyone
called her a tomboy, but such names meant nothing to
me. I have a strong suspicion that it was she who gave
me the make- up kit. I can't remember if I painted my
face with any of the contents, but the mere possession
of such a thing was enough to raise my parents' hackles.
Oh my, what an inquisition it caused! 'Where did yaw
get that from?' and 'Who gave it to yaw?' My father ordered my mother to 'take that thing from 'im', and then,
in a voice of great solemnity, said to me: 'Dow yaw ever
let me see yaw with anythin' like that agin'.' Well, he
didn't. That was the last I saw of the make-up kit and
my parents never mentioned it again. How different
things are today. The only man I can remember who
wore make-up in those days was Coco the Clown. Now,
thanks to the likes of Boy George and all who followed,
anything goes.

* * *

It seemed as if I was not like other boys in a physical
way either. For some reason, my testicles did not descend into my scrotum shortly before birth, as normally
happens, but neither I nor my parents became aware of
this until I was ten years old. My parents were very
prudish and ill-informed about sexual matters. My

10

mother, having had only sisters, was not aware of how boys developed, although she must have seen me when I was born. I can only speculate that my 'un-boyish' behaviour raised questions in my parents' minds as to my gender and physical development. When it finally dawned on my mother that something might be wrong 'down below', she became very agitated and took me to see her mother, who was none the wiser. Together they peered at my penis, which hung in isolation without any sign of testicles. My genitals were discussed in muted tones and I was eventually taken to the local doctor. He duly referred me to a specialist, who confirmed that I did in fact have testicles, but that they were still in the abdomen. He assured my mother that they would descend in due course and that there was nothing to worry about. They did just that and gave me no further trouble. I developed in the normal way and entered puberty two years later, but the incident still left me with a nagging sense of shame and unease.

* * *

Another consequence of my non-conformity was that I never belonged to a gang – I was always the odd man out. However, there was one occasion when Norman and I, along with our cousin, Billy, clubbed together to smoke our fathers' nub ends. For a half penny, we bought clay pipes and a bag of sherbet with a dip stick of liquorice from the sweet shop, then roamed the waste ground around our homes until we found a dug-out where we could smoke our pipes away from preying eyes. It was not long before we felt sick as dogs, so we returned home and sheepishly asked if we could go to bed. Mother was very suspicious and interrogated us about why we suddenly wanted to go to bed. We never told her what we had been up to. Mind you, it probably put a stop to smoking later in life. In the Navy I smoked a pipe until the novelty wore off, but other than that all I ever smoked was a few menthol cigarettes to take away the pain when my father died.

* * *

Throughout my childhood and early teens my unusual behaviour manifested itself in many ways but was perhaps most evident in the hobbies and pastimes I pursued compared to those of my brother. At Christmas, we were given lead soldiers, cowboys and Indians, and farmyard animals, but I always claimed the farmyard animals. I was not interested in shootin' and playing at 'Cowboys and Injuns'. Instead of aggressive games such as marbles, conkers and fives, I was more interested in spinning tops, knitting and corking (spool knitting), although I did play Tiddlywinks, Ludo, Snap and later Monopoly. We were forbidden to have playing cards because of their association with gambling and addiction. Norman's main interests lay in mechanical things – especially trains – and later in motorbikes and cars. His love of trains has remained with him all his life; even today at the grand old age of eighty-nine his spare bedroom is full of track, miniature rolling stock and mockups of the countryside. We did, however, share a great enthusiasm for plasticine clay, modelling houses and men and anything else required for our storylines. My brother's men would go off on expeditions and adventures, then return to my place to have a meal and rest.

12

Perhaps all this explains why we both remain firm fans of *Wallace and Gromit!*

My hobbies changed over time: drawing and painting everything I came across gave way to making marionette dolls. They were made from string, wool, matchsticks and any odd bits of material I could find in mother's sewing box and father's tool shed. In our small kitchen, my brother and I had special places for our toys and hobbies. Norman's was on the wooden top which covered the boiler used for heating the water for wash day. This dreaded ritual took place every Monday and if the weather was bad so was my mother's mood. Norman and I didn't like wash day much either because it meant nothing but cold food and hard work: we had to fold the sheets meticulously and then put them through the mangle, controlling them as they emerged on the other side. Next, we had to peg them on the clothes line – and woe betide us if we let any part of the sheets touch the ground! My special place for my toys and hobbies was the back of a cupboard in the far corner of the kitchen, on which I pinned my drawings and paintings around a cardboard theatre proscenium arch. Here, I would also exhibit my marionette dolls. This always caused my father to raise his eyebrows, although I seem to recall that he was intrigued with the dolls' construction, especially their working parts and controls. My mother called our assortment of toys 'Tranklements', which I later discovered was a word peculiar to the Black Country, used to describe ornaments and bits and bobs.

My parents were also alarmed at my interest in drama, although they never made their reasons clear. Maybe they wanted to protect me from the perceived loose morals of theatrical types or thought that my involvement might incur expenses they could not afford. I am sure they also felt that the theatre was 'above my station' and not for the likes of poor people. In any event, my acting debut was not auspicious. In junior school I was given the part of Cobweb, a fairy servant to Titania the fairy queen, in an adaptation of Shakespeare's *A Midsummer Night's Dream*. I only had one word to say, but I blew it by appearing on stage at the wrong cue. I don't remember any repercussions from my father on that occasion, but I doubt whether he would have been interested enough to attend the performance.

Ironically, it was my father who played an inadvertent but important role in strengthening my fascination for drama. Due to a long illness, which I will describe in more detail later, my father had been unable to work for ten years. However, when WWII broke out in September 1939, he signed himself 'off "the box" (the sick list)' against his doctor's advice and returned to his job in the electrical industry, which was now focused on war work.

This upturn in my parents' fortunes enabled them to afford a holiday, so they took my brother and me to Colwyn Bay, a seaside resort in North Wales. This was a rare treat as annual holidays had hitherto been limited to a day out on a charabanc to a seaside resort or a pleasure park. On this occasion, we were joined by my mother's sister and husband – Aunty Ivy and Uncle Bill

14

– and their son, my cousin Billy, who were regular visitors to Colwyn Bay. Apart from the beach, our favourite place was Eirias Park where there were putting greens, a miniature golf course, and a boating lake. One day Uncle Bill, whom I liked very much and who had encouraged me to swim, suggested taking us boys on the boats, but I did not want to go. Secretly I found rowing a bit of a problem as it was difficult to negotiate the oars, especially as you had to sit facing the opposite direction to that in which the boat was moving. So, I was reluctantly left to my own devices. In the distance, I saw a marquee with rows of deck chairs in front of it. As I approached, I could hear voices and wondered what was going on. I discovered that there was a play in progress. I had no money, of course, but I managed to crouch between some deck chairs within the enclosure without being spotted. I was spellbound, so enraptured that I lost all sense of time. Although unsure what the play was or what it was about, I was gripped by the dialogue, the actors, their costumes and the scenery. The next day I saw on the park notice that it was Shakespeare's *The Merchant of Venice* that I had been watching. I recalled having read an abridged version of the play from Charles and Mary Lamb's *Tales from Shakespeare*, a book I had stolen from school! When my parents ultimately found me, they were beside themselves with worry and anger as they had almost given me up for lost. There were stern words of warning from my mother and a customary slap around the ears from my father. But it was worth it: what a discovery! Afterwards, there was quite a lot of ragging about my theatre escapade. I had caused my parents much anxiety by wandering off, but I also think they felt I was becoming a bit of a snob by aping middle class cultural interests.

My mother's disapproval of the theatre did not end there: two further occasions spring to mind from when I was in my late teens. My mother's younger sister Aunty Iris lived with my grandmother Gray while her husband, a Regimental Sergeant Major in the regular army, was away on war service. She invited me to accompany her to the theatre. I don't recall the play, but when I told my mother she said, 'Certainly not, I won't let yaw goo with 'er.' I assume that she thought my aunt, who had been known to have dalliances with other men, was a bit flighty; and, as I was growing into a handsome but very naïve youth, my mother did not trust her to keep me on the straight and narrow. The other occasion was when a colleague at work invited me to the theatre. Again, my mother refused to let me go. My employer had taken on a German Jew, named Fritz Wertimer, who had escaped with his father from Nazi Germany.

I suspect that my mother thought I was too young to be going out with an older man, especially a Jew and a German at that! I seem to recollect that there was a certain amount of prejudice against Jews and Catholics amongst my family in those days. When my Uncle Cyril, my father's younger brother, married Kitty who was a Roman Catholic, there was a lot of bad feeling in the family about their marriage, mainly because my grandfather was a staunch member of the Church of England. They also disapproved of Catholics because they did not practise birth control and consequently brought children into the world whom they could not afford to bring up properly.

Although my parents' prejudice against the arts never wavered, I did win the battle in the end. Before I was conscripted into the Navy at the age of eighteen, I managed to see Daphne du Maurier's *Rebecca* at the Theatre Royal in Birmingham, George Bernard Shaw's *Pygmalion* in Hansworth Park and many plays at the Birmingham Repertory Theatre. I have enjoyed the theatre all my life and it has given me so much pleasure. In my retirement, I was for a time honorary treasurer for the Vic-Wells Association which promotes opera, drama and the ballet in the Old Vic and Sadler's Wells theatres.

* * *

My 'differentness' also manifested itself in my interest in ballet dancing. I made friends with the two children of my Sunday School Superintendent. Gordon was about my age and his sister Alma slightly younger. I was often invited for Sunday tea at their house, where I felt accepted and loved for the first time in my life. Mr and Mrs Knott and their children seemed to be a truly loving family whom I envied very much, especially because they talked to each other. After Sunday School the three of us would go to West Smethwick Park, near our homes. The land had been given to the community by Chance Brothers, manufacturers of lighthouse glass amongst other things, which had become part of the conglomerate of Black Country industries. Alma went to ballet classes and she loved to show off to her brother and me the classical moves and the steps she was being

17

taught. I was fascinated and tried to imitate her, although by this time I was losing the suppleness which children have, and I struggled with some of the more tortuous movements.

When the film *Billy Elliot* was released in 2000, it was a joy to see the breaking down of prejudice against ballet in the culture in which Billy was brought up. I don't think the same could ever have happened with my parents. Fortunately, they were unaware of my interest in ballet and never found out. There was one occasion, however, when my mother caught me dancing around the room in a style akin to that of Isadora Duncan, the American dancer and choreographer. My mother thought I was quite mad. In my twenties I went to ballroom dancing classes, which came in useful when I attended dinner dances arranged by my accountancy professional body. When I moved to London in my thirties, I went to Cecil Sharp House in Primrose Hill to learn folk dancing; later, I attended yoga classes where I once met the actress Sheila Hancock. These activities were beyond the critical eyes of my parents as I had by then long flown the nest. I have loved dancing and the ballet ever since.

Chapter 3

STICKS AND STONES

Sticks and stones may break my bones, but names will never hurt me. Don't you believe it. It all hurts, and the scars outside and inside last a lifetime.

It was a Sunday morning when it first happened. I was about eight at the time. After attending the morning service at the Methodist Church, I used to go and see my grandparents who lived nearby. Walking down Barker Street to their house I saw in the distance someone ambling towards me. As the figure came nearer, I could see it was a boy named Barry Groves, who was older and much bigger than me. He was swaying from side to side, determined that no one should get past him without a collision. The closer he came, the more threatened I felt.

I wanted to make a run for it, but he was determined to keep me in his sights. Our bodies clashed, and his punch sent me sprawling on the pavement. I heard him burst out laughing and caught a glimpse of him running up the street waving his arms in the air, triumphant at flooring his latest victim.

I managed to pick myself up, recovered my cap, which I found in the gutter some yards away, and ran like the clappers up the dark passage to Grandfather Gray's house at number 93. I burst into the living room and stood there, trembling like a leaf. 'What's up wif yaw?' asked my grandfather in his Black Country brogue. He

19

was sitting at the dining room table while my grandmother was putting the back stud in the white starched collar and shirt that she had just ironed. Grandfather was dressing up in his Sunday Best to go for his usual drink before dinner at the Bell Inn, the public house at the other end of Barker Street. I mumbled something about being punched by Barry Groves in the street and grandfather said, 'Why, yaw am big enough to ate 'im', his way of saying that I was big enough to eat him, although this was plainly not the case. With that grandfather finished dressing, complete with waistcoat, into which he put his Half Hunter gold watch and chain, gave me my weekly penny pocket money and left us. As he went through the side door into the dark passage, I heard my grandmother shout, 'Bob, dow yaw be late for yer dinna!' I also beat a hasty retreat, anxious to shadow my grandfather for protection just in case there was another sighting of the bully.

I did not call to see my other Grandfather Underhill that morning, even though he only lived a few doors away from Grandfather Gray, but went home another way. It took longer to walk, but I felt safe. I never said a word to my mother or father about what had happened. In any case, I was too ashamed of myself and my father would only have called me a big sissy for not standing up for myself. Years later my brother confessed to me that he had also been beaten by the notorious bully of Barker Street, who lived midway between our two grandfathers' houses. He also admitted to being bullied at school, but he never shared this knowledge when we were young. Thereafter, whenever I visited my

20

grandparents I did so with some trepidation and kept a keen eye for any sign of danger. If I spotted the bully, I would dash past him or turn on my heels and find some place to hide until the danger had passed.

* * *

Barry Groves was not my only tormentor. In fact, I was bullied throughout my time at school. When my mother took me to Bristnall Hall Elementary School at the age of five, I burst into tears and would not leave her – not an unusual reaction for a child on their first day at school – but even though I soon stopped crying, the event set the tone for the rest of my school days.

The curriculum was very basic: it included woodwork and metal work, but was bereft of the classics, modern languages, music or science. The school tried to teach higher maths, which I could never grasp; I still wonder what practical use trigonometry and algebra would have been in our humble lives. Corporal punishment was administered freely, and I was on the receiving end on several occasions. My ears were pulled by the primary teacher because I could not distinguish the letter 'Y' from the word 'why'. My brother likewise suffered from this lady. She used to pull his ears too, but because he suffered from chilblains on his ears in the winter, she made them bleed! I was caned by the maths teacher for not doing my schoolwork on higher maths and hit across both hands with a Bunsen burner hose by the craft teacher for a misdemeanour I do not recall.

Constant bullying from other boys, which I endured without telling a soul, undermined my confidence and made me lonelier than ever. Consequently, my school work suffered. The education system made no provision for the late developer. There was little in the way of progress assessments, and so I left school at the age of fourteen without any certification.

Some of the older boys often lay in wait for me on my way from school. After a tussle, I'd escape and run home hell for leather or avoid them by taking another route. But it was the playground where I was most vulnerable. At playtime I would make myself scarce by finding a secluded place to hide or hang around at the edge of a gang of boys hoping that I would not be spotted. I remember one occasion when this strategy failed me. As I stood there minding my own business, I became aware that there was some sort of confrontation taking place at the centre of the gang. To my horror, a gentle and well-spoken boy with whom I was slightly acquainted was being cajoled into putting up his fists and fight another boy. I could not bear the sight of this inoffensive boy being provoked in such a way and before I knew it, I was pushing my way through the crowd.

'Leave 'im alone. He doesn't want to fight yaw,' I said to the bully.

'Oh, and who do yaw fink yaw am? Stick up yer fists,' he answered.

'No, I don't want to fight yaw either. I don't believe in it,' was my reply.

'Goo on, fight 'im,' shouted the other boys.

'No,' I insisted.

'Yaw yella, big sissy,' they shouted back at me.

At that moment, the school bell rang and we all returned to our classes, but I was in no state to concentrate on what the teacher was saying. I was still trembling from my encounter with those bullies and wondering how I could get home in one piece.

I never did learn how to defend myself like Tom Brown did against that horror Flashman in *Tom Brown's School Days*, even though I had been given the book by a teacher as a prize for good work when I was in the junior school. Consequently, I am still puzzled why I acted out of character and stuck up for the boy who was being made to fight, even though I could not stand up for myself. Perhaps it had something to do with my growing awareness of the teachings of Jesus Christ, about whom I had learned at Sunday School. I was captivated by the portrayal of Jesus in the Gospels as a man who resisted tribal instincts and defended the underdog – the finest example of the altruistic gene. However, it was listening to *The Man Born to be King*, a radio drama by Dorothy L. Sayers, that really inspired me to take Jesus as a role model. While there was an outcry against the BBC at the time for broadcasting the voice of Christ, the play was ground-breaking in the way it dramatised human emotions and motivations not always explicit from Gospel records. In bringing the story of Jesus alive, it made a strong impression on me. So much so, in fact, that I secretly asked Him to be my friend and guide in life. These two events – listening to the play and standing up for that boy in the playground

– marked the beginning of my Christian journey of faith.

* * *

One of the things which caused me great anxiety and led to another kind of bullying was my ineptness at and dislike of sport. I recall, for instance, when Grandfather Gray took me to see the local football team, West Bromwich Albion, at the Hawthorns. The team was known as 'The Baggies', a name derived from the baggy shorts the players used to wear in the early days of the club. I was totally bored, but to please my grandfather I tried to raise a cheer when they scored a goal. I was made to play football at school, but I was so lacking in co-ordination or aggression that I was soon demoted to the reserves. To be honest, I never did see the point of kicking a bag of wind about.

I was bad enough at football but when it came to cricket, of which my father was very fond, I was a total disaster. In the first place, I was terrified of the hard ball. I remember that my mother was once hit in the eye with it while watching us in the local park. When father sent me out to bat, I simply couldn't connect willow with leather and hardly ever scored a run. As for fielding, I could neither catch the ball nor throw it to the bowler. My eyes never saw it coming and my arms could not get the hang of projecting it with any semblance of direction or distance. I can still hear my father's humiliating jibe – the all too familiar, 'Yaw big sissy' – at my inability to perform. No one was ever kind or patient enough to give me any advice or encouragement; everyone seemed to assume that the ability to handle a bat and ball or kick

24

a football around came naturally because you were a boy. On the other hand, I was quite good in the gym and at swimming, which I have enjoyed all my life. In my twenties, I also played a lot of table tennis and lawn tennis. I tried golf too, but all I did was uproot the turf!

* * *

My closing year at junior school was marked by a great disappointment. In the thirties, there was an opportunity for promising children attending elementary state schools to apply for places at the local grammar school, but selection was by external examination. There were no mock examinations like they have today. You had one chance and that was it. In any event, I had been upgraded from the 'B' to the 'A' stream of classes and so was considered eligible to take the exams. Like a lamb to the slaughter I went along to the grammar school and sat papers on English, maths and general knowledge. I failed to meet the standard required.

The names of the successful children were read out by the headmaster during morning assembly and my name was not among them. Some of the other kids laughed and jeered when they heard I had not passed the examination – served me right for thinking that I was cleverer than they were! To rub salt into the wound, I did not get the school tie which my Aunty Ivy had promised me if I passed.

All this meant that I had to go up into the senior school and continue to encounter the bullies who had terrified me in the past. Furthermore, it gave me no choice but to leave school on my fourteenth birthday and go out to work. The biggest humiliation, however, was being snubbed by the mother of my best friend, Derek. After the results were announced I called on Derek, who had passed the examination, to come out to play. His mother greeted me with the words, 'Derek won't be playing with you any more as he will be making new friends when he goes to the grammar school.' Many years later I told my mother this story and she was very hurt as she knew Mrs Waterhouse through the local Baptist Church, which they both attended. Again, I was a disappointment to my parents and suffered another blow to my self-esteem because I was not good at sport or academics, or so it seemed.

* * *

My young mind was always alert to the threat from my aggressors at school, but in the great scheme of things the biggest bully of them all was Germany. Britain entered WWII not long after I moved up into the senior school. My schooling was interrupted for a while so that an air raid shelter could be erected in the school playground. Our home was also supplied with an Anderson air raid shelter which my brother and I helped my father to install at the bottom of the garden by the gooseberry bushes – where, according to the old wives' tale, my brother and I had been brought into the world. A great hole in the ground had to be dug before the shelter could be assembled and put into the ground. We were issued with gas masks and identity cards. All road signs were covered up and curtains made from black material had to be hung at every window so that the 'blackout' could be enforced. All street lighting was forbidden, and the centre of towns, shops and cinemas lay in total darkness during the curfew between dusk and sunrise. The Home Guard was formed, a civil part-time army conscripted to guard and patrol key locations throughout the land, also Air Raid Protection Wardens (the ARP) were also recruited to help people during the air raids. Factory workers had to do Fire Watch duties after their shift, staying on to look out for incendiary bombs dropped by enemy aircraft. This was why my father sometimes would not return home from his work until the following day. Young teachers at my school who had been called up were replaced by older men who came out of retirement.

When rationing was imposed in January 1940, we were allowed only 2 oz. of butter, 8 oz. of sugar and 2 oz. of cheese per person per week. Less essential foods were subjected to a points system, although we did receive new foodstuffs from America such as dried egg and pineapple jam, which I found very tasty - although I soon got very sick of Spam meat.

While life in the armed forces during the war was unimaginably tough and dangerous, there were times when life for us civilians was hard too. My family was still very poor, and my mother always shopped in the town centres where fruit and vegetables were a penny or two cheaper than in the local shops. Forays into town involved walking up to three miles to the shops, where I often queued for hours in the freezing cold. By the time it was my turn to be served there was sometimes nothing left, so I'd have to make another trek the next day.

The days were a grind, but our nights were an entirely different and often a traumatic experience because of the air raids. At the sound of the sirens we'd abandon our beds and rush to the air raid shelter, armed with our gas masks and bedding. The shelter in winter was freezing and sometimes waterlogged, and it made me feel very claustrophobic. I was experiencing puberty at the time and so used to comfort myself by masturbating! It wasn't long before the family grew sick of these nightly upheavals, so in the winter months we'd simply huddle under the kitchen table instead of dashing to the shelter.

Our morale was constantly shaken by Lord Haw-Haw – real name William Joyce – who broadcast propaganda for the Germans from their medium wave station in Hamburg. His programme always opened with the words, delivered in a sinister nasal twang, 'Germany calling, Germany calling.' On one occasion he remarked that 'Germany had not forgotten little Oldbury,' implying that the Luftwaffe would bomb the town where we lived as this was where munitions and poisonous gas were being made for the war effort. No tears were shed when Joyce was hung for treason after the war.

One night while we were in the shelter there was an almighty explosion in the next street to ours. It transpired that a German plane had been shot down by the anti-aircraft gun – nicknamed 'Big Bertha' – stationed at Turner's Hill in nearby Rowley Regis. The plane demolished two houses and wrecked another, killing all the occupants and the pilot. Aside from the 'ack-ack' guns, part of the national defence system included barrage balloons which kept aircraft from flying low and thus made it much more difficult for them to aim accurately at targets. There were two barrage balloons quite near to where we lived, one of which was on the allotments behind our school. Here there were also searchlights which tracked the bombers and picked them out as targets for the anti-aircraft guns. One night a strong wind blew one of the barrage balloons from its moorings and the cable ripped off the roofs of nearby houses. Eventually the balloon had to be shot down before it caused further damage.

The final method of defence was the smoke drums on street corners. When ignited, these sent clouds of smoke into the air to confuse the bombers. When there was no wind a dark cloud from the factory chimneys always hung over the valley, affording some protection from the bombers that were seeking to destroy them. Nevertheless, neighbouring towns like West Bromwich and Wolverhampton suffered heavily at the hands of the Luftwaffe, while Birmingham some five miles away was one of the most heavily bombed cities in the UK. August 1941 saw the first bombing raids on the city of Birmingham. I vividly remember standing with my brother at our bedroom window and watching the old market hall in the Bullring as it burnt down after being set ablaze by incendiary bombs. Twenty-five people were killed that night.

* * *

I returned to school after the air raid shelter was finished but despite all the fear, excitement and upheaval the war had brought to our community, there were still boys around who were game to pick a fight – and they'd often pick those fights with me, especially on my way home from school.

What I needed was something else to occupy my mind. Such a diversion came to me in a form I least expected. I'm not sure how the school obtained a printing press and all the equipment necessary to print our own publications. Nor am I sure how I came to be selected to learn how to operate the press. However, I took to it like a duck to water and spent much of my time away from classes perfecting the process and printing material for distribution. One of the projects in which I was engaged was a *History of Oldbury*, for which I designed the cover. I cut a lino block showing the factory scene with which I was so familiar. I can recall drawing the outline of the tall chimney stacks, the round gasometers, the canal bridges and the tiny back-to-back houses sandwiched between the factories. My work was widely praised and gave me a much-needed sense of satisfaction at a time when I was very unhappy. It was because of this project that I was invited by the boss of a printing works to join as an apprentice compositor rather than having to go into a factory on war work. But more of my experience as a printer anon.

* * *

How I came to have two sets of boxing gloves, I don't remember. However, I was keen to have a go and invited Kenny, the boy who lived next door, to spar with me. He came from a family of four children and was about my age. We were having a knockabout in our backyard when my mother came out to see what I was doing. Horrified, she immediately put a stop to our boxing bout and made us take the gloves off. I never saw them again. She was not going to let her son engage in such a rough sport – I might get hurt! Little did she know the good it might have done me. It might have given me the courage to stand up for myself against those bullies at school who constantly tormented me.

Today people and institutions are much more aware of the problems caused by bullying, but it still goes on and always will, particularly now that the internet has given bullies free rein to vent their spleens. In any event, I believe that the problem can never be solved entirely by others; and if I could meet my younger self now, I would teach him the art of self-defence so that he could engage his adversaries in a way they'd never forget.

I was still bullied from time to time right up until the age of fourteen, when I had to leave school and go out to work. I never told my teachers or my parents or confided in my brother about the bullying. An appeal to my parents would have been useless anyway: my father would only have called me 'yaw big sissy.'

The emotional scars of being bullied – whether sticks, stones, or names – have undoubtedly had a lasting effect on my life. It certainly inhibited my progress at school and left me solitary and insecure. I tended to be diffident and lacked self-confidence. Little wonder that self-esteem, which is so essential to becoming a mature adult, had little chance of developing. In later life when circumstances pushed me into the public domain, I had a battle royal with my shyness and poor self-image. I found it very difficult to hold my own when faced with aggressive and manipulative people, especially when I came up against them in the workplace. It was a long journey before I could confront my demons and choose 'fight' instead of 'flight'.

Chapter 4

TOM, TALK TO THE BOY

My father, Thomas Henry Underhill, was born in 1904 at Catshill, a village just outside Bromsgrove in Worcestershire, the eldest son of Henry and Sarah Underhill. When my father was still an infant the family moved to Oldbury, where my grandfather got a job at Chance Brothers, who made glass for lighthouses. My father met my mother because she lived in a house only a few doors away. She remembered him as a 'smart-looking chap with jet black hair.' He was twenty-two and she was just twenty-one when they married in November 1926, by which time I was already well on my way. Having a child 'out of wedlock' was simply not the done thing in those days, so my parents had no choice but to get married – and this had many repercussions.

Conversation with my father, if you could call it that, was virtually confined to commands to do something – 'Time yaw was in bed' – or some reprimand – 'Big-un (being the older son), yaw ought to 'ave known betta.' If my brother and I got into any sort of trouble I was always held to blame. I remember when, for example, my brother and I were caught engraving our initials on a tree in the local park with the penknives we'd been given for Christmas. The park keeper confiscated our knives. When my father found out he blamed me entirely, even though both of us were caught leaving our mark for posterity.

The fact that my father hardly ever spoke to me apart from imperatives or reprimands was difficult to bear. I complained to my brother about it, but he did not see any problem as he had a good relationship with father. When I broached the subject with mother, she explained his behaviour this way: 'When yaw brother was a few weeks old your further was taken bad. 'e spent two years confined to 'is bed and a district nurse come to the 'ouse daily to dress 'is wounds and tend to 'is business. Whilst further was bed-ridden 'e looked after your brother because I was overwhelmed with looking after yaw, a babe in arms and a sick mon.' As she frequently used to say, 'I 'ad to be mother and further to all three of yaw.' I suppose in modern speak she was referring to the 'bonding' which obviously took place between my father and my baby brother, but I had missed out on all that.

Although my mother tried to intervene now and then – 'Tom, talk to the boy', she pleaded – the alienation got worse over the years. I dreaded the occasions when mother had to go into hospital, first for the removal of gallstones and then for the removal of a goitre in her neck. Later, she had to have her tear ducts removed because they had become infected and finally, she had a hysterectomy. On these occasions, when father was left in charge of us, I felt as if I was orphaned with no one to talk to. The imperatives and reprimands continued apace, but there was hardly ever any real conversation.

As my mother often commented, my father's problem was that he was 'ignorant and devoid of emotion,' a criticism she also made against other members of his

34

family; especially his father. My father just could not understand why I did not conform to type. The strange things I did, my inability to play games and my artistic interests appeared to him girlish rather than masculine. This is not surprising as the prevailing culture was a very macho and stiff upper lip one, where men did not cry or show their emotions. Empathy was not a word in their vocabulary and it was a long time before I learnt what it meant. My father never hugged or kissed anyone, nor did I ever witness any kind of physical affection between my parents. He would have had no understanding that his son might be homosexual, as the word did not even enter common parlance until much later in the century. The nearest he ever got to it was the word 'sissy'.

The expectations at that time were that a boy should grow up to be like his father and follow his trade or profession. My burgeoning interest in drama and the arts obviously alarmed my parents because careers in the theatre and the arts were precarious and offered no security.

As I did not conform to their expectations, they were both disappointed and anxious. Instead of saying 'Oh, isn't 'e like uncle Joe' or 'Don't 'e take after your Grandfurther Gray,' my mother used to say to me, 'I don't know where yaw came from or where yaw get these strange ideas from. Yaw don't take after any of us.' Well, if I was not an Underhill nor a Gray, then who was I then?

Quite late in life I read that extraordinary story *Alice's Adventures in Wonderland* by Charles Dodgson. In the second chapter, Alice finds herself down a rabbit hole having drunk something which made her grow first very tall and then very small. She begins to cry and is soon drowning in a pool of her own tears. After a strange conversation with herself about who she might be, she says:

"If I'm like Mabel (one of her school friends) I will stay down the hole: it will be no use putting their heads down and saying, come up again, dear". I shall only look up and say, "Who am I then? Tell me that first, and then, if I like being that person, I'll come up: if not, I'll stay down here till I'm somebody else."

I have spent too much of my life down my own rabbit hole. It was a long time before I knew who I was and an even longer time before I could love who I was. Rejection by my father, society, and the Church made self-acceptance very difficult indeed and left me with a lot of self-hate. There was a long and tortuous journey ahead of me before I could respond to the command of Jesus: 'you shall love your neighbour as yourself' (Matthew 19:19b).

* * *

It must not be thought that my father was a bad man. One thing he possessed more than anything else was courage – or as he would have put it, 'guts'. When he was twenty-four, he had an operation to remove an abscess from his abdomen which went wrong and ultimately became tubercular. He overheard the specialist telling my mother 'I give him six months,' and afterwards, when he had left, said to my mother, 'I'll show 'im'. He defied this prognosis, living until a month before he was sixty-five when he died of cancer of the small intestine. After spending two years confined to his bed, he started to get about again, doing odd jobs for people. He built a greenhouse and grew tomatoes which he sold to friends and neighbours. At the outbreak of WWII, he threw caution to the wind and against his doctor's advice got a job at Joseph Lucas, manufacturers of electrical parts for cars and machinery, which by then had been commandeered for the war effort. He worked for the rest of his life, which was punctuated with short spells in hospital. Two virtues which he had in abundance were stoicism and patience: despite the pain and discomfort he suffered for much of his life, I never once heard him complain about his health; and he was extremely patient with my mother whose anxiety – or 'nerves', as she called them – often drove him and the rest of us mad.

My father smoked and drank modestly as there was little money for such things. He was competent at his trade as an electrical engineer and could take a car engine to bits and put it back together again. I never heard him crack a joke but there was one saying of his which I found very funny. Come rain or shine, when not at work he would always wear thick woollen underwear underneath a suit with a waistcoat, shirt and tie. During the summer months or on holiday I would ask him if he was hot with all those clothes on. His reply would always be: 'What keeps the cold out, keeps the 'eat out!'. Following trials with the antibiotic Streptomycin from 1946-47, my father's wound partially healed. This must have been a great relief because ever since his operation in 1929 he had had to endure an open wound in his abdomen, which often leaked. This gave off an unpleasant smell which he used to try and mask with cheap perfume.

I can hardly imagine the frustration and disappointment that father must have suffered as a young married man because he could not go out to work and support his family. What money my father had when first married went on doctors' fees. All my mother had for a household comprising of a sick husband and two small children was a means tested allowance of 28 shillings a week (£1.40p in decimal currency). In those days means testing was extremely rigorous and very intrusive; their capital had been spent on specialist fees and being not long married there was nothing of value in the house which could to be confiscated. I suspect that my parents regretted my brother's arrival because his birth coincided with my father first being taken ill. Determined not to have any more children because we simply could not afford it meant that my mother denied my father a normal sex life, which left him even more frustrated.

* * *

One day my father, my brother and I made kites out of old newspaper, bits of wood and string, glued together with flour paste. We then went to nearby Barnford Hill Park, where there was some high ground known as 'Pudding Rock' and flew our kites. A strong wind was blowing that day, so our kite flying was a great success. Sadly, that remains the only happy occasion whilst I was a boy that I can remember sharing with my father.

My father rather than affirming or encouraging me, often laughed at me instead. One of the things which irritated him most was when he found me reading the books I had borrowed from the local library. 'Got yaw 'ed stuck in a book agin?' he would scoff. 'Get off yaw backside and do summat useful!'

In contrast my mother, on winter nights, would read to us from the books we received as Sunday School prizes. She was also very fond of reciting to us from Oberon's famous monologue in A Midsummer Night's Dream from Act 2, Scene 1. It was sheer magic. Even today I can still recall the sound of her voice reading these words.

> I know a bank where the wild thyme blows,
> Where oxlips and the nodding violet grows,
> Quite over-canopied with luscious woodbine,
> With sweet musk-roses and with eglantine:
> There sleeps Titania sometimes of the night,
> Lull'd in these flowers with dances and delight;
> And there the snake throws her enamell'd skin,
> Weed wide enough to wrap a fairy in.

But there was no such connection with my father. In fact, I don't remember him or any of our relatives ever reading a book. There were certainly no books to be found in their houses. We were too poor to buy the children's books which were popular when I was young, like *Winnie the Pooh* or *The Wind in the Willows*. Although my school put on a production of *Toad of Toad Hall*, an adaptation of *The Wind in the Willows*, and we read *The Children of the New Forest* in class, I had not realised what I had missed until I discovered the magic of such classics much later in life.

Of course, my father's disdain for books was hardly surprising considering his own father could not read at all, leaving school when he was only nine years old and working as a farm labourer for a large part of his life. In psychological terms, my father failed to validate me as a person, deprived me of love, and led me to believe that I was unfit for purpose. There is no doubt that his rejection of me contributed to my mother's overprotectiveness, the subject of my next chapter. I can only conclude that my father was ignorant of the harm he did to me. The central tenet of Christianity is forgiveness, taken from a Greek word *aphiemi*, meaning 'to let go, release'. This I have tried to do. Although I don't hold it against my father anymore, I cannot forget the way he treated me. Even now, I can hear my mother pleading to him, 'Tom, talk to the boy.' But he never did. Couldn't, wouldn't, who knows?

My relationship with my father improved in later life, and this helped to heal the rift of those early years. During my accountancy training and when I moved to London, I returned home to see my parents on special occasions. Sometimes I joined them and my brother and his wife on holiday, usually in Wales. When my father's youngest sister, Matilda (Aunt Tilly) moved to Horsham because of her husband's work, I joined my family in regular visits to see them and their two adopted children. My parents even came to London to stay with me in the terrible flat I rented in Chelsea. On all these occasions, it was obvious that my father's attitude towards me had softened. He had lost all his old hostility and treated me with respect. Gradually we began to talk to each other, and he showed some interest in my life, especially when I left the firm of accountants I was working for and started up on my own account.

It was during this period that his old bowel condition flared up. He was admitted to the Queen Elizabeth Hospital in Birmingham. I was shocked when I saw him in hospital as they had him on a machine which was draining his insides. He died there from cancer of the small intestine in March 1969, just before his sixty-fifth birthday. I was very sad that after all he had suffered in his younger days, he did not live to enjoy his retirement, and that we did not have the chance to get to know each other better.

Chapter 5

MOTHER SUPERIOR

My mother was born in 1905 and baptised Florence Phyllis Gray after her mother Florence Gray, who was always called 'Florie' by her husband Robert Gray. So as not to cause confusion with her mother she was called 'Phyl' by my father and the family. She was the eldest of four girls (my grandmother's first daughter, Lily, died soon after her birth). A photograph taken of my mother when she was sixteen shows that she was an extremely pretty girl, a fact that my father cannot have missed when she moved in a few doors down the street.

From an early age, my mother was made to take responsibility for running the household and caring for her sisters. Becoming pregnant with me at the age of twenty-one left her with no choice but to marry my father. While this at least offered some escape from her very demanding mother, it was really a case of out of the frying pan and into the fire: soon she would be faced with looking after two young sons and a sick husband with hardly any money at all.

My mother loved my brother and me, of that there is no doubt. But she could never really let us go and sought to control our lives in ways that often caused us great frustration. Although she was a nervous person – and became increasingly so as she grew older – she was also strict and, at times, truly formidable. Woe betide you if you did things she did not like or if you disobeyed her rules.

Yet my mother was, in many ways, an extraordinary woman. She was the second of five girls, but when the first daughter died mother became the eldest. Her own mother had a car accident – rare in those days – and was virtually scalped as a car drove on with her hair caught in the bodywork. The shock of the accident took away my grandmother's confidence and my mother found herself running the household and virtually bringing up her youngest sister, Winifred, single-handed.

To make ends meet during WWI, her father built a candle-making machine in the shed at the bottom of their garden. Even though she was only in her early teens, my mother was put straight to work, producing high-quality candles and selling them to local shops for about tuppence a bundle of twelve. She also had to take a wheelbarrow to the canal depot to collect the slabs of pure white candle wax brought by barges from places where the fat had been rendered down and purified. Little did my mother know that her hard life at home with her parents would be good training for her future.

Of course, cottage industries were widespread in those days. Old Hill, not far from where my grandparents lived, was famous for brewing, chain-making and nail-making. My sister-in-law Doreen remembers her grandmother making nails in her backyard from rods of iron, hammering them into shape with the aid of wooden blocks while on her knees. Some 12 lbs of iron rods would make 10 lbs of nails for which she would receive one shilling and a half penny – slave labour to be sure, but it enabled the family to make ends meet.

* * *

My mother's expectations of a happy married life faded when, within just two years of marriage, my father fell ill and was unable to work. She was indeed both father and mother to my brother and me while we were growing up. In addition to running our household of four on a pittance, mother repaired our boots, cut our hair and made our short trousers, pyjamas and shirts from off-cuts she bought at the market, aided by the Singer sewing machine that my grandmother gave to her. She even knitted our socks, jumpers, gloves and scarves. When we needed formal clothes for events like our Sunday School anniversaries, she bought hand-me-downs from rich families. Every so often an elderly woman, Mrs Wilson, would appear at the front door laden with bags stuffed with second-hand children's clothes. Mother would shoo us boys into the kitchen and order us not to disturb her while she cast her eye over Mrs Wilson's offerings. When the special occasion arrived mother would produce these clothes, newly washed and ironed. My brother and I would be dressed in beautiful boys' blouses (slightly dressier than shirts), short cotton socks instead of the rough, long woollen socks we normally had to wear and, best of all, what I called 'low shoes'. I hated the black boots that we normally wore. They were such a job to lace up properly and they used to hurt my ankles; what's more, they made a noise when you walked due to the metal tips hammered into the heels and toes so that the soles would last longer.

As well as being practical and industrious, my mother was also artistic. In addition to reading to us on winter nights she taught my brother and me to play the piano, and when my father returned to work, she sent me for piano lessons. We inherited our piano from my mother's parents – the same one she used to play to entertain the relatives when they visited my grandparents' home for a swell meal and a sing-song – occasions which inevitably ended in a row if the booze flowed too freely. When she could afford it, mother occasionally bought second-hand sheet music of popular songs from market stalls at a penny or two per copy. She would then sing the songs to us and teach us the music. One thing she could not stand, however, were arias from operas. She said they upset her, I think because she could not cope with their passionate intensity. People in those days were buttoned-up emotionally and did not show their feelings. My mother was no exception. Indeed, I cannot recall witnessing any displays of emotion such as hugging, kissing, embracing or expressions of affection by either of my parents or any of my relatives. Apart from my Aunty Ivy and Uncle Bill, they were a very cold lot. As I once heard my mother complain about her in-laws: 'Them Underhill's, they got no feelings, yaw know!'

My mother had a good writing hand, and during my time in the Forces she wrote to me long and well-expressed letters. She was equally good with numbers, and when it came to money, she took her accounting very seriously. After shopping she would do her 'reckoning up', as she called it, and if she could not account for every penny, she would worry herself sick. Perhaps her obsession with getting her maths right had some influence upon me becoming an accountant. She was strict to the point of paranoia about borrowing money or having anything 'on tick' or 'on the slate'. Despite her antipathy towards the theatre, she was always quoting to us from Shakespeare especially Hamlet, and Polonius's advice to Laertes: 'Neither a borrower, nor a lender be, for loan oft loses both itself and friend, and borrowing dulls the edge of husbandry.'

I have often reflected that if she had had the opportunity she would have gone to university, but she was wasted by the pressures upon her to serve as a workhorse, first for her parents and then for her own family. My mother became a drudge for my father's family too, especially for his sisters Ella and Tilly, who could neither sew nor mend. After she had reared my brother and me, my mother was inundated with requests for making curtains, altering clothes and mending socks for 'Uncle Tom Cobley and all, and all for just a few coppers.'

* * *

In those days, it was a moral disgrace to bear a child out of wedlock. So much so, in fact, that women who fell pregnant before they were married were often put into institutions for corrective care. When I was a Member of the Society of Saint Francis, I became 'a friend' to a group of people who were released into the community from St. Augustine's Hospital, a former county asylum near Canterbury. Among them was a woman in her forties who had been sent there for having a child out of wedlock. She had become so institutionalised that she was unable to manage her own affairs, so my job was to help her until she had the confidence to look after herself and live independently.

That experience often made me think of my mother because she too conceived her first child – yours truly – out of wedlock. What traumas and recriminations this caused at the time I cannot say. All I know is that my parents had no choice but to get married before I was born to avoid disgrace. For this reason alone, it was not a match made in heaven, but I suspect from things my mother said in later life that this would have been the case whatever the circumstances. One of her favourite idiomatic sayings on this matter was: 'As you make your bed, so you must lie on it.' There was never any romantic talk and she never even mentioned her wedding anniversary, let alone celebrated it. I only discovered the actual date when I came across the marriage certificate after my mother died in September 1992, just before her eighty-seventh birthday.

Marriage did at least enable her to get away from her mother, who treated her badly. Grandmother never forgave her for marrying, and she certainly had little time for my father especially as he had taken away her skivvy, which became obvious from the family rows I witnessed as a child.

* * *

This portrait of my mother would not be complete without mention of her religious faith. Although she was brought up as a Methodist, the constant workload of her domestic duties left her little time to attend church or Sunday School. Throughout our childhood, she came to our Sunday School anniversaries at the local Methodist church, when we were dressed in our Sunday best and sang hymns for our parents on a platform hoisted over the Communion Table. Later in life she attended the local Baptist church, and when she came to live with me after I was ordained in the Church of England, she became a regular worshipper wherever I happened to be. She came to a deeper understanding of her faith in the fifties when Billy Graham, the American Evangelist, brought his crusades to this country. We used to have long philosophical discussions as to why God permitted innocent people to suffer while the faithless seemingly prospered.

Despite my mother's sensitive and thoughtful nature, I never told her of my unhappiness over my sexuality or about my terrible depressions – she had suffered enough in her life without my adding to it. Nevertheless, I got the feeling that she knew I was homosexual and accepted it. She was always very friendly and complimentary about the friends I brought home later in life, especially James, who has been my friend for the last fifty years. In May 2018, he celebrated his ninety-sixth birthday. Nor did I ever confront her about the way she stifled my interests and tried to control my life, which on reflection, deprived me of much of the joy and freedom of simply being myself. Her refusal to let me go hindered the process of finding my own identity.

She was, for all kinds of reasons, a worrier. I used to say to her, 'If you had nothing to worry about, you'd worry that you had nothing to worry about' – to which she would reply, 'Yaw don't know what I'ave bin through.'

49

For a long time, I thought she was referring to the hardships of bringing up two children with no money and a sick, disillusioned husband, but increasingly I began to realise that other factors were involved. It was only when I was writing about my grandmother that it dawned on me that much of her anxiety and misery was caused by the treatment she received from her mother and, later in life, the hurtful things she suffered at the hands of my Aunty Win, her youngest sister whom she virtually brought up single-handed. Back then, people who were anxious and plagued with doubts were said to be suffering from 'their nerves', rather than the pathologies that would be diagnosed today. Sadly, as my mother grew older, she became more and more anxious until she reached a point where no one could reassure her. To some extent, I think I am 'a chip off the old block' – as one of John Milton's poems has it – and have inherited some of my mother's anxiety, but of course for different reasons.

Chapter 6

OVERPROTECTED AND OVER POSSESSED

I think that I was nine years old and still in junior school when we were taken for swimming lessons at a new open-air swimming pool. I was worried because each session cost tuppence and with so little money coming in, I didn't think my parents would be able to afford it.

As things turned out, this was not the main obstacle. 'Yaw'll catch yaw death of cold,' my mother warned, insisting that I was 'not a strong boy.' Wanting so much to learn to swim and finding water attractive, I pleaded with her to let me go. After a lot of arguments and no doubt some tears, she relented. I soon got my orange stripe for swimming the length of the pool. I have continued to swim all my life and it has been a real joy. But if I hadn't made such a fuss, things might have been very different: while some parents throw their children in at the deep end, others are reluctant to let them even dip a toe in the water. My mother came from the latter camp.

Looking back, I think my mother's overprotectiveness of me was rooted in my very beginning: when I was born, I weighed only four pounds, which was very small for a male child (I could possibly have been born prematurely). I was, according to my mother, such a 'delicate baby' that she had to nurse me with special care and wash me in olive oil. I could not take her milk, so instead of breastfeeding she had to give me Cow & Gate formula. All of this made her anxious and worried right from the start – and this became a habit that never left her.

* * *

When I was about eleven, I got hold of a scooter. How I don't know, because my parents certainly could not have afforded to buy me one. On examining the scooter, I discovered that the back wheel was adrift, so I rummaged in my father's shed and found a huge nail which made do as an axle. The nail had to be bent to secure the wheel, and I did this by striking it with the coal hammer. Once I'd made my repairs, I scooted off down the hill to see my grandparents and aunts. I loved every minute of it, but my freedom was short-lived: when my mother saw that I'd worn a great hole in the sole of my right boot, she put an end to my scootering right away.

With the scooter gone my next passion was to buy a second-hand bicycle, so I began to save furiously. I got a penny a week from my Grandfather Gray and a half-crown from him at Christmas. My cousin Billy received pocket money from his parents, but I don't remember mine giving us any; however, I did earn some money from my father by collecting horse manure. In those days there were still horse-drawn vehicles on the roads, and my father used the manure as fertiliser for his tomatoes. He gave me sixpence for each barrow load. I was embarrassed to be shovelling manure so I used to go to the streets where I would not be recognised, but I needed the money. At last I saved the required amount

– 12 shillings and sixpence – to buy a second-hand bicycle.

Mr Jukes and his family lived next door but one to us. My brother used to call for their middle son John to go to school together. One morning he was invited into the house as John was not quite ready, only to find John's two younger sisters sitting naked at the kitchen table and dipping pieces of dry bread into a bowl of tomato ketchup – presumably their breakfast. Mr Jukes, who it transpired had just been released from prison for theft, was not popular with our neighbours because he grazed his goats in his back garden and sometimes in theirs too! Anyway, my brother also learned that Mr Jukes' brother, who lived nearby, ran a second-hand bicycle business. This was music to my ears as I was dead set on acquiring a bicycle.

When I told my mother of my intentions she flew into a rage: 'If yaw bring that bike 'ere I shall put the 'ommer through it. Just yaw wait until yaw further comes 'ome!' Her fury was understandable because it was a bicycle accident that caused her husband to be invalided for ten years with only a frugal state allowance for support. In desperation, I appealed to my mother's younger sister, Aunty Ivy, who persuaded my mother to let me bring the machine home. Mind you, it was a terrible bike. There was always something going wrong with it – it was made up entirely of spare parts, many of which had to be replaced within a short time. Mr Jukes got fed up with me asking for replacements. The frame was too big for my height, but no one thought of lowering the saddle; consequently, every time I fell off it, which in the early days was quite often, I hurt my genitals. I nick-named my bike '57 Varieties' after the famous Heinz advertising slogan. Fortunately, my mother's fears were not realised, and I became an enthusiastic cyclist. The bike proved to be a great asset in my teens, especially when I went out to work. I used to cycle to Birmingham every day, a round trip of twelve miles. I was in great demand and my parents and relatives sent me on countless errands, but I also cycled for pleasure, often exploring the lovely Worcestershire countryside.

My mother was similarly overprotective of my brother, although not to the same extent. While I was working in Mansfield, my brother did his National Service in the Army Catering Corp. After his demobilisation he bought a motorbike to travel to work and back. My mother simply went berserk: she remonstrated, she pleaded, and when all else failed, she threatened that if he had an accident she would not look after him. To mitigate my mother's anxiety, my brother would turn off the motorbike's engine when he returned late at night before he got to the house and then free wheeled the bike to the house, so that if my mother was in bed she would not hear him come home. Despite such precautionary measures, my mother remained bitterly opposed to the motorbike and their relationship was strained for a long time.

* * *

During the period when my father was unable to work, he took a correspondence course with Bennett College of Sheffield and obtained a qualification in Electrical Engineering – he also made our first wireless set. It was

54

a little more sophisticated than a crystal set (cat's whisker receiver), which required no electricity or accumulator but simply picked up signals from an antenna, but it needed certain materials which, sadly, became unobtainable during the war. I remember vividly the day the wireless finally gave up the ghost for lack of these materials. My brother and I were trying to listen to 'Toy Town', part of a programme called *Children's Hour*. It was broadcast every week day between 5 and 6 pm by the BBC Home Service. Mother got very angry with us for straining so hard to listen. She said we would damage our ears and she turned the thing off. For me, however, the loss of the wireless was a great deprivation and I shed many tears over it.

I was becoming very aware of the great difference in the language spoken by the announcers on the BBC and that which my family and neighbours spoke. The dialect we spoke in the Black Country retained the short vowel sounds from Anglo Saxon and Middle English. It also dropped the 'h' from words – for instance, the local workhouse Hallam House was always pronounced 'Alla Mouse'. In addition, the region had its own unique vocabulary: if you got drunk you were 'kalied'; if you were in good health you were 'bostin'. 'Keep out th'oss road' meant 'mind how you go'. I could certainly hear the differences between the language of the Black Country and the BBC, but I lived such an insular life at the time that I did not realise people in other parts of the country spoke in different dialects. When Aunt Tilly, my father's youngest sister, got married and moved to Horsham in Sussex, the shopkeepers could not understand her at all. Michael, her adopted son, told me years later that his dad always did the shopping because she was too embarrassed.

I wanted to be understood by people who lived in other parts of the country, so I started to imitate the BBC announcers. 'Oo, 'ark at 'im,' mocked my family, 'ain't 'e talkin' posh!' But I wasn't trying to be posh and it wasn't that I disliked the way we spoke, even though it often sounded ugly to my ears; no, it was just that if I ever left the Black Country, I didn't want to suffer the same fate as Aunt Tilly.

We had to wait until father resumed work before he could buy a more sophisticated wireless set, which ran off an accumulator. Even then it had to be recharged every week at the local radio shop because we only had gas lighting. On a lighter note, I should mention that we used to love listening to Francis Durbridge's serial 'Send for Paul Temple', with Peter Coke playing the great detective. In 1945 my mother's school friend, Margery Westbury, took the part of Steve, Paul Temple's wife. My parents used to visit Margery Westbury at her home somewhere in the Worcestershire countryside and were apparently made very welcome. Mother must have been a very close friend of Margery to look her up, but she would never have reciprocated by entertaining any acquaintance at home. She was too ashamed of our poverty.

* * *

As well as being overprotective my mother was also over-possessive. This caused me further mental conflict and inhibited me from doing things and going places.

Two occasions later in life stick in my mind and I relate them now, even though they break the sequence of this narrative.

The first occasion was in January 1948 when I was de-mobilised from the Royal Navy. I returned briefly to the Black Country where my parents still lived, and where my previous job as a compositor in the printing trade was being kept open for me. While serving in the Royal Navy I met another SBA (Sick Berth Attendant), whose name was Alex. His father was a practising accountant who had offered me a job as a clerk in his office in Mans-field, Nottinghamshire, and an opportunity to study for the accountancy examinations. In those days, the pro-fession could only be entered by being articled to an ac-countant who usually required the payment of a pre-mium of 100 guineas or more, and without salary for the term of the articles. Such an opportunity was not to be missed if I was to fulfil my ambition to qualify as an accountant and avoid badly paid factory work, which I loathed. So, within a few days I left for Mansfield. My mother was very upset. 'After all we've done for yaw and now yaw is going to leave us,' she complained, a re-proach I heard from her many times. I don't think she ever forgave me for leaving home. She simply hated the idea of change, believing that you should stick to the same job for ever. That old saying attributed to Publil-ius Syrus, a former Syrian slave and Latin writer – 'a rolling stone gathers no moss' – was never far from her lips. I suppose this was an indication of her own insecu-rity, borne of her own broken dreams. She exerted sim-ilar pressure on my brother when he wanted to move to Scotland to take a better paid job in the printing trade.

She prevailed, and my brother has regretted it ever since – he stayed with a local firm which did not adapt to the new technology and which ultimately went out of business. My brother called it 'emotional blackmail'.

The second occasion when I experienced again the full power of 'mother care' was in 1956, when I returned to the Black Country after spending eight years away in Mansfield training for my accountancy qualification. The decision to live with my parents again was not an easy one, but my mental breakdown and subsequent hospitalisation made it difficult to continue living in Mansfield. My parents met the resident psychiatrist on my discharge from the mental hospital and were told some harsh truths about their parenting skills. This seemed to have some effect on my father, who lost the hostility he once had towards me. Afterwards we began slowly to talk to each other. But it made no difference as far as my mother was concerned. You would have thought that during those years in which I had flown the nest she might have lost the habit of trying to control my life, but not a bit of it. Even though I was nearly thirty, she insisted that I be in the house by ten o'clock each evening because she said that she could not go to sleep unless she knew I was at home. Furthermore, she would not allow me to bring any friends home – not even John, our next-door neighbours' eldest son, who was about my age and had some mental problems. A year later my mother happened to be in the back garden when John came out of the house and shot himself while she looked on in absolute horror.

By the same token my mother would not invite home any of the friends she met at the local Baptist Church. She said that she did not want them to see 'what 'er 'ad'. This puzzled me because my parents were still relatively poor and had nothing to boast about in terms of possessions. As a child, I was never allowed to bring friends home: my mother's reason then was that we could hardly feed ourselves, let alone someone else's children. My brother and I were never given birthday parties like our cousin Billy.

Her last prohibition during my return was that I could not do anything which made a mess. She did not like the house to be untidy or in a muddle, so that put an end to my forays into DIY even though I was good at it. Granted, the house was so small you could hardly swing a cat round in any of the rooms. It was the second council house my parents had rented. This one had electricity, whereas the house in which I grew up only had gas. But it had an outside toilet like that of my grandparents' houses and to my astonishment my parents were still using torn up sheets of newspaper on a string, apparently still unable to afford toilet rolls. The back door opened directly on to the backyard, letting all the warmth escape from the only heat source which was a small coal fire in the kitchen. Towards the end of my stay, I did at least persuade my mother to let me erect a kind of lean-to, to protect them from the cold and rain when they used the toilet.

After a year of living with my parents I had had enough of apron string rules. My anxiety over my sexuality was as bad as ever, so I was recommended to see a Freudian psychoanalyst. This entailed moving to London and, despite my precarious mental state, I couldn't leave fast enough.

Chapter 7

THE FACTS OF LIFE

Ignorance of the facts of life caused me no end of grief. The onset of puberty was a complete mystery to me and I thought I was becoming seriously ill. During the war my mother preserved eggs in isinglass, a preservative made from a part of dried fish. I used to dissolve the isinglass in water and drink it in the hope that it would cure me of whatever was happening to me. My father's youngest brother had died of a mastoid when he was twenty-one, so I claimed I had one too as a ruse to get myself examined by a doctor who would then, I hoped, diagnose what was really wrong with me. The doctor confirmed that there was no mastoid, but sadly did not spot my deception or that I was anxious about the changes taking place in my body.

My first inklings of puberty began when my brother and I romped around on the bed and I felt a stirring in my loins, which resulted in a feeling of exhilaration and excitement. Curiously enough, my brother and I experienced it at the same time and we coined a phrase for this: 'feeling tough'. I asked him if he wanted to feel my penis, but he did not. I reckon I was about twelve at the time, so he would have been ten. The next stirring occurred some days later when I felt my penis become erect. I was near the stairs which led up to the bedrooms. Instead of stimulating my penis with my hand, I lay with my belly on the stairs and rubbed my penis on the edge of the steps until I ejaculated. Although it was an exhilarating experience, I felt that I had done something terribly wrong and wished that it had never happened.

*　*　*

The idea that 'children should be seen and not heard' – a saying attributed to a fifteenth-century Augustinian monk originally aimed only at girls – was very much in vogue in the culture in which I grew up. Despite Queen Victoria's love of sex, the repressed sexuality of that period still dominated. Any questions we asked about sex or babies were met with a 'never yaw mind.' My parents were prudish in the extreme and ignorant about sexual matters. The only phrase my mother ever used that had anything to do with sex was 'the curse'. It was not until years later that I understood that she was referring to her monthly periods, which were always a trouble for her before she had a hysterectomy. There was no hope of getting any fatherly advice about sex as we hardly ever exchanged a word. There was no sex education at school either, nor did I get the usual initiation in sexual matters or experiences of mutual masturbation in the toilets with my peers at school as I kept my distance from other boys, especially those who bullied me.

I had never seen my father naked. In fact, the only time I ever saw a naked man was in the school showers. Just before the outbreak of WWII the local authority built a gymnasium on part of the playground at my school. From then onwards we had physical training (PT) lessons in the gym, after which we showered. I remember seeing that one of the teachers who showered with us had an erection and I found the sight somewhat scary.

62

I don't recall that there was any misbehaviour, but I was so naïve about such matters I would not have understood anyway. Old wives' tales about sex were still legion, the most ridiculous being that I was born 'under a gooseberry bush', of which there were several at the bottom of our back garden. I have since looked up this strange saying on the internet and found that it was not so strange after all as it referred to the pubic hair. Thus, naïve in the extreme at the age of fourteen, I went out to work for my living not knowing the facts of life. Philip Larkin famously said that 'Sexual intercourse began in nineteen sixty-three' but I'm sorry to say that this was much too late for me!

* * *

The first time I remember being attracted to the male body was when I was learning how to swim. Our instructor, who also taught wood and metal work at my school, took some of the older boys for diving lessons. The sight of his body when he dived was exhilarating to watch. My earliest pin-up was Buster Crabbe, who starred in the first space movie *Flash Gordon's Trip to Mars*. The film was shown in instalments at our local cinema, the Regent Palace. My brother and I called it 'The Flea Pit' as the air after the performance reeked of the smell of not-so-clean children. The usherettes used to go around the place with a spray containing lavender scented water to get rid of the stink.

I found my next sex idol in *The Sunday People*, one of the newspapers passed on to us by relatives, which included an advert depicting Charles Atlas (real name Angelo Siciliano) saying, 'You too can have a body like mine.' His method of body-building was called 'Dynamic Tension', a form of callisthenics. This passion for developing his muscles arose out of being bullied on a beach and being laughed at by his girlfriends. With my track record of being bullied, his story certainly hit home. I wrote away for his course, but my mother spotted the reply and confiscated it.

I explored my growing attraction to the male form in magazines imported from North America. I bought them from a dubious bookshop on Cape Hill, which I passed twice a day on my way to and from work at the printers in Birmingham. They included colour photographs of handsome young men in posing slips, on the pretext of encouraging fitness and health. Such magazines provided gay men with at least some means of stimulation and pleasure, as human contact was, of course, a criminal offence (full nudity could not be published until after 1960). I suppose they were the forerunners of what we now call 'gay porn'. I tried to hide the magazines at home, but my brother found them and showed them to my mother. She made no comment but, true to form, the magazines disappeared, and I never saw them again.

Despite my attraction to the male body – which, in a more enlightened age would suggest that I was homosexual – I fell madly in love with Ethel, known to everybody as Et as she did not like her baptismal name. We met at the Methodist Chapel where I had worshipped since I was a boy. The problem was that she was ten years my senior and this did not go down well with my parents. They pointed out that when I was fifty she

64

would be an 'old woman' of sixty, adding that the days when I would be able to earn enough money to support a wife were a long way off – and back then, the idea of a husband being kept by his wife was unacceptable.

Et had a wonderful personality and was very physically attractive. She had a lovely voice and I used to accompany her on the piano when she sang classical arias from operas. Her favourite songs were 'One Fine Day' from Puccini's *Madame Butterfly* and 'To A Wild Rose' by Edward MacDowell. Et's parents accepted me without any apparent problem. Her mother was a good dressmaker who made many of her daughter's clothes. Her father, who had retired, was a staunch Labour supporter with whom I shared my socialist aspirations. Et was the head cashier at Cox & Danks, an iron and steel scrap merchants with a depot in Langley not far from where she lived. The business was responsible for breaking up some of Germany's naval fleet after WWI.

I was very taken with her and we spent quite a time on her front doorstep kissing and cuddling passionately. I was certainly in love with her and I'm sure my feelings would have found physical expression had not sex before marriage been so taboo. Add to this the fact that we were both church-goers – and my own naivety about the mechanics of conception – and I can report that kissing and cuddling were as far as things ever went.

We used to go cycling a lot, often making forays into the beautiful Worcestershire countryside. On one occasion we cycled out to the River Severn near Bewdley to a well-known beauty spot called the Black Rock. I wanted to show Et my swimming skills, and in so doing I nearly drowned. It was Easter and the river water was still very cold, but I stripped off, dived in and began swimming toward the opposite bank. Halfway across I was overcome by the cold and lost control. I distinctly heard a voice say to me 'lie on your back'. I did and began to float down the river until I finally found myself in shallow water amongst the reeds. Et, who had seen my plight, waded into the river but as she could not swim, she started calling for help. Fortunately, there was a scout group camping on the opposite bank of the river. They heard her cries and a scout came in a canoe and rescued us, then took us back to the camp and gave us tea and comfort! To this day, I cannot identify the voice that spoke to me! This was not the first time that I had a near-death experience, but more on that anon.

* * *

My affair with Et continued for about two years until I was doing my Sick Berth Attendant (Nurse) training at a commandeered psychiatric hospital in Barrow Gurney, not far from Bristol. There, I met another conscript who was about to marry a girlfriend who was also ten years his senior. Despite this confirmation that I was not the only one involved with an older girl, I suddenly decided to call off my relationship with Et. At home on leave in 1946, I broke the news to the families, causing consternation in both households. Et was heartbroken and her parents were very disappointed; my parents less so because of the difference in our ages. To this day, I don't know why I ended the relationship. All I know is that my feelings for Et changed and I no longer felt emotionally involved with her. Many years later, after my

66

mental breakdown, I consulted a Freudian psychoanalyst about my behaviour with Et. His theory was that I was drawn to her as a mother substitute rather than as a lover. Whether he was right, I just don't know. Long after our affair, my mother met Et by chance and learnt that she was about to get married for the first time. According to my mother, Et, who must have been about forty by then, seemed rather anxious about the whole thing, but more than that she would not say. I hope for all kinds of reasons that she had the happiest of marriages.

Philip Larkin summarised my anger and frustration at my parents for bringing me up without any guidance about the facts of life when he said, 'They fuck you up, your mum and dad. They may not mean to, but they do.'

Chapter 8

THAT SLAVE DRIVER

It is a well-known fact that nurture is just as important as nature in determining who we become in adult life. In both respects, our parents have a great influence on us, for good or bad. I've spent many years trying to un-ravel why my mother was such a bag of nerves all her life. Undoubtedly her marriage was a great disappoint-ment to her, but I think the seeds of her anxiety were sown by her own mother.

My grandmother, Phyllis Cartwright, was born into a well-heeled family who owned a safe-making business. Her brothers fought in WWI and afterwards emigrated to Australia and Canada because there was no employ-ment for them here. My mother recalls being taken in a hansom cab with her sister Ivy to stay with their grand-parents – a big house where they slept in a four-poster bed. I believe that there were some domestic staff too.

My grandmother met Robert Gray, her future husband, at the Methodist Chapel in West Bromwich where they later married. My grandfather passed on to me his Sun-day School prizes – huge volumes of stories about un-fortunate people being rescued from the follies of drink and gambling and then brought to God. Such salutary tales clearly had no lasting influence as my grandpar-ents severed all connections with the church after they married, and were very critical of my mother who sent my brother and me to the Methodist Church at the top of their street. Grandfather Gray drank heavily, and grandmother was not far behind. So was my father's younger brother, Cyril, who married a Roman Catholic lady; he spent most of his spare time at the public house called The Barrel near to his home. Grandmother obviously felt she had married beneath herself, and the shabby house in Barker Street in which she spent her married life was a constant reminder of this fact. She rued the hard life that resulted from marrying a poorer man and resented looking after her four young daughters – as well as the humdrum household chores this entailed. My mother, the eldest child, became grandmother's skivvy – responsible for running the household and caring for her three younger sisters. No wonder my mother always referred to grandmother as 'that slave driver'.

* * *

My mother often complained about her mother not letting her go out to work like her sister, Ivy, who was a couple of years younger. Ivy was allowed to work at Parke's Classical Sweet factory, which was virtually on the doorstep. There she met the man she married, William, a sugar boiler. I liked Uncle Bill; he took an interest in me and I was envious of my cousin Billy for having such a lovely dad.

Mother always blamed grandmother for keeping her at home because it deprived her of the opportunity to experience life outside the domestic environment, particularly when it came to meeting young men. She wanted to get a job to improve our finances during the ten years that my father was ill, but the opportunities denied her in younger life meant that she lacked the confidence to do so.

Then, of course, there was grandmother's meanness – she paid my mother the princely sum of sixpence per week for staying at home and doing all the work! My mother recalled saving up those sixpences to buy a pair of silk stockings, the height of fashion in those days, particularly as the hemlines of dresses had been raised high enough to show off women's legs.

When mother was twenty-one, she met my father, known as Tom, who lived only a few doors away. When she fell pregnant it did not go down at all well with grandmother. Quite apart from the disgrace, it meant that she no longer had someone to do all the household chores. Even then she still made my mother and her sister Ivy clean her house once a week, despite the fact that they were married and had their own families to look after.

But it was my father who bore the brunt of grandmother's wrath. She never forgave him for getting my mother pregnant and often treated him with disdain. My brother remembers one unhappy occasion when all the family were at my grandmother's house for a Christmas drink. Grandmother gave each of her three sons-in-law (my uncles) a 10-shilling note but did not give one to my father, even though he was the least well-off having been out of work for so long because of his illness. You can imagine the hurt this caused!

On another occasion my grandmother gave my brother and his wife an egg and a bar of soap for their Christmas present, adding that they certainly needed the soap. This was definitely a case of the pot calling the kettle black as I don't think she had had a bath for years since there were no bathing facilities in her house. The truth is, I'm afraid to say, that grandmother was a mean and spiteful woman.

* * *

My grandmother took in lodgers now and then to make ends meet, usually businessmen who had found employment in the area. I remember one in particular: Mr Jones, a well-spoken, well-educated bachelor. When I first saw him, I clearly remember wondering how such a nice man could have taken lodgings with such an awful woman in such a terrible house. My grandmother wasted no time in trying to marry off her fine gentleman lodger to father's eldest sister, my Aunty Ella, but neither party was interested. Why Aunty Ella turned down so many suitors was the subject of much debate in our family. My mother, never one to mince her words, put it down to the fact that she was 'stuck up'.

Grandmother, who was an awful gossip and very nosy, somehow got wind of a story that Mr Jones had been stripped naked by his colleagues at work and then tarred and feathered. What prompted such barbaric treatment remained a mystery, but the effect must have been devastating on grandmother's shy and cultured lodger. In my naivety, I had no idea of the significance of tarring and feathering, although I discovered later that the practice became rampant during the American Civil War as a mob action of public humiliation. The next time I heard the expression was in the film *My Fair*

Lady where Eliza's father sings 'I'm Getting Married in the Morning' and invites his pals to 'feather and tar him' on the eve of his nuptials!

Before Mr Jones left Barker Street, he invited my brother and me to his family home in Colwell Green; a village just outside the lovely market town of Ledbury in Herefordshire. One Sunday morning in late autumn the two of us duly set off on our bicycles and cycled to Colwell Green, the furthest we'd ever penetrated the delightful countryside that lay to the west of the Black Country. We were treated to a lovely meal by Mr Jones' family, who then stuffed our pannier bags with Cox's apples, Victoria plums and William pears from their orchard to take home to our mother. The journey home was very slow and hard-going and we were still on the road when dusk descended. The war was still being fought, so we soon found ourselves cycling in total darkness because of the blackout and discovered to our horror that the batteries in our headlamps had run flat. I knew there was a bicycle shop in Romsley, a hill village about eight miles from home, but being a Sunday, it was closed. However, we alerted the owner and he kindly opened the shop and sold us the batteries we needed (fortunately we had some money on us, which was very unusual!). We were dog-tired by the time we arrived home, but also the proud possessors of delicious, fresh fruit from the countryside. The next day my mother took some of the fruit to my grandmother at which point she flew off the handle, insisting that *all* the fruit was *hers* because Mr Jones was *her* lodger!

* * *

There is a story dating from my mother's teenage years that she told us many times. It seems my grandfather was rather too fond of the ladies who frequented the pub he visited every Sunday. One night he stayed out until very late. When he finally returned, an almighty row ensued during which my grandmother hurled her wedding and engagement rings into the fire. Upstairs in bed, my mother and her three sisters lay shaking in terror at the commotion going on beneath them. They thought there was going to be a murder! The next morning, my mother was ordered to rake through the ashes and retrieve the rings.

While my mother lived in fear of grandmother's tantrums, she always had a soft spot for her father despite his bad habits. Sadly, grandfather drank heavily and died of cirrhosis of the liver when he was fifty-six. He always said that he wanted 'a happy life, but a short one', but only half his wish came true. After his death, grandmother became even more scathing about her two eldest daughters if they neglected her in any way.

* * *

As a teenager I used to visit my grandmother quite often, more out of a sense of duty than pleasure. There she'd sit at the dining room table, pince-nez on her nose and a stub of a pencil in her hand, pouring over The *Pink'un* – published by the *Birmingham Evening Post* – studying form (the track record of the winners and who was the favourite for the 2 o'clock race). She would write down on a scrap of paper the names of the horses on which she wished to place bets. Then there'd be a knock on the door and a runner would take the note and her stake money. Later, the runner would return to the side door and put her winnings – if any – with a note under the door. She was quite a lucky gambler. Rather than hiding her winnings under the bed as most people did in those days, she sewed the money into her voluminous petticoats for safe keeping.

Grandmother liked a drink too. From an early age, I was commandeered to fetch her stout from the off-licence at the top of the road, directly opposite the Methodist Church I attended. I was terrified that someone would recognise me carrying the jug of beer down Barker Street because I had 'signed the pledge' not to touch alcohol. Grandmother would sit in front of the fire to drink her stout, occasionally plunging a hot poker into the jug so that the stout would bubble up to the top. Woe betide anyone if they interrupted her drinking routine. Such an intrusion would elicit a torrent of very ugly words – words I never heard from either of my parents.

The other thing that put me off visiting my grandmother was the reek of the winter-green oil with which she anointed her body to ease her 'rheumatics'. Perhaps if she had got off her bottom and done some housework she might not have felt so stiff or been such a moaner about her pains!

* * *

As is the way of things, grandmother lived to quite a ripe old age. She died in her bed, wearing the very petticoats she'd stuffed with all her gambling money! I always thought of her as a bit of a dragon, and now I see her as the main reason why my mother was such a nervous wreck.

Whenever I think of grandmother's death, I am immediately reminded of my Aunty Iris, one of mother's younger sisters. My mother referred to her as 'the black sheep of the family' because in her younger days she had dalliances with other men and was always borrowing money from grandmother, which she never paid back. Aunty Iris was the first daughter to arrive at grandmother's deathbed. My mother came later, only to find that the petticoats had been rifled and the bank notes had gone. Also, a memo signed by my grandmother regarding the rest of her money appeared to have been tampered with, giving priority to Aunty Iris. Furthermore, she had laid out the corpse for the undertakers and inserted pennies into her eye sockets. Aunty Iris admitted nothing. The 'doctored' memo was the subject of a six-year legal wrangle before the issue was finally resolved. In the words of the solicitor, 'Mrs Holyoak [Aunty Iris] has considered the matter and graciously agreed to give a third share of their late mother's estate to each of her two sisters [that is, my mother and Aunty Ivy].' Aunty Win, the fourth and youngest sister was not included in the hand-out because she had severed all connections with the family many years before. Despite her faults, my grandmother certainly had the measure of her daughter Iris. Her repeated warning to us went like this: 'Yaw want to watch 'er. Er's a bugger', although I still don't believe she knew what the word 'bugger' really meant.

Chapter 9

WICKED AUNTY WIN

Winifred 'Win' Gray, my mother's youngest sister, married Christopher Gunn – a very tall and overweight Master Butcher who ran his own shop with Win as his assistant. They never had any children of their own, but during the early years of their marriage Chris's two younger brothers lived with them as their own home had been broken up. As soon as they were able and found suitable employment, they fled the nest. On Sunday mornings after church my brother and I used to call on them and take their dog for a walk, for which we were given a penny. Aunty Win was always cheerful, but Uncle Chris rarely uttered anything but sarcastic remarks – a habit he maintained even with his own customers!

The incident that caused all contact between the Gray family and the Gunn family to cease occurred in the early part of WWII. Aunty Iris – the black sheep of the family – was staying at my grandmother's house with her Sergeant Major husband, Bill Holyoak, who was on leave from the Army. According to my brother, who happened to be visiting our grandparents at the time, things turned nasty when Uncle Chris called round to deliver some meat – a rare commodity at the time because of rationing. Uncle Bill, who was also very tall and strong with a voice that could wake the dead, decided this was the time to confront his brother-in-law: 'Why are yaw not in the Army,' he challenged, 'fightin' for yaw country?' Fisticuffs ensued. Uncle Chris fled the scene and never put a foot in his mother-in-law's house again – and neither did Aunty Win. I understand that Master Butchers were exempt from National Service, but Uncle Bill would have none of it. We were forbidden to mention the incident and never allowed to visit Aunty Win or Uncle Chris again.

* * *

Aunty Win made no attempt to contact any of her family for the next forty years. Then one day she just turned up on my mother's doorstep, hoping to resume their friendship. My mother had been widowed for some years by then, but Win had only recently been widowed, her husband having died of leukaemia. She had sold the old rambling house we used to visit as children and bought a smaller, detached modern house not far from my mother's. It seems that Uncle Chris had left her well provided for because she bought the new house for £13,000 in cash!

It was not long before my mother was making the curtains for Win's new house while my brother replaced the old fire grates with modern ones and fitted a new front door. For my mother, it was like old times again – doing the bidding of exploitative relatives for a pittance. When Aunty Win had to have her knees replaced because of her arthritis, it was my mother and brother who ended up serving as carers during her hospitalisation and convalescence, even though she had gone private! No aftercare is one of the downsides of private medicine!

Aunty Win became very much part of the family again. At the time I was a team vicar at St. Aiden's, Cannock, not far from where my family lived, so I saw quite a lot of them during my three-year stay. Aunty Win, my mother, my brother and his wife Doreen were frequent guests at the vicarage for birthdays, Christmas and bank holidays. On one occasion Doreen brought along an old friend, Jane, whom she had met many years ago when they worked together at a factory which re-threaded car tyres. Jane was in a very distressed state and after our meal, she asked if she could have a private chat with me so we retired to the study while my guests drank their coffee. Her story was heartbreaking. Unbeknownst to her, her husband Jack, a heavy drinker, had been persuaded by his drinking pals to drive a vehicle containing drugs to a particular destination and then leave them there, a tactic deployed to put the police off the scent. Unfortunately, two of the men involved in the plan had accidentally switched on a baby alarm while staying at a hotel and their entire conversation had been overheard by the receptionist, who had immediately reported the matter to the police. All those involved in the drug run were rounded up and arrested. Jack was found guilty of carrying drugs and sentenced to five years in prison. Jack was a good husband but easily led astray, and the havoc he caused was far-reaching: his marriage was on the brink, his children were ashamed and embarrassed, and he'd left Jane in dire financial straits.

When we re-joined the party, Aunty Win's curiosity got the better of her. 'What's up with 'er then?' she queried. 'Er's what?' she exploded, on hearing of Jane's misfortunes. 'Er ought to be ashamed of 'erself!' There are no words to describe such insensitivity. Despite Aunty Win being told that it was none of her business, she simply would not shut up. Norman and Doreen had no choice but to take Jane home.

* * *

Over the years, widowed Aunty Win kept in touch with the wives of various business associates in the butchery trade. But more often than not she was always at loggerheads with them or embroiled in some acrimonious telephone conversation which ended in her slamming down the phone. Another of Aunty Win's friends was Peggy, the widow of Sydney Grayland, the sub-postmaster of the local sub-post office who was the third man to be murdered by the 'The Black Panther' alias Donald Neilson. Peggy was also injured during the robbery of the Post Office and was taken to the mortuary as she was thought to be dead. However, she regained consciousness whilst in the mortuary to the utter astonishment of everybody concerned. Some thirty years later these terrible events still played on Peggy's mind and at times life was very difficult. No matter, if she offended Aunty Win in any way down would go the handset. Whenever I enquired why she wasn't speaking to Peggy or Joyce or whoever, the reason my aunt gave always seemed very trivial. It seemed to me that Winnie had no capacity for empathy or understanding of other people's difficulties and took offence if anyone threatened her in any way. After a few weeks of silence, she would ring up the offending party as if nothing had happened and the whole saga would be repeated.

Aunty Win never needed an excuse to take umbrage; witness the time she was invited to stay with her friends Gerald and Jean, who owned a farm near Bridgenorth in Shropshire. Win thought she was going for a holiday, so when she was asked if she minded washing the eggs before they were taken to market, she was so affronted that she immediately packed her case and got the train back to Langley Green.

Knowing what Aunty Win was like, I should have thought twice before I introduced her to a friend of mine, a widower whom I had met on holiday and who lived quite near her. He visited Win quite regularly and as she became more immobile, he used to transport her to the hospital for her physiotherapy sessions. One day her front door would not open. Rather than acknowledging that the lock had simply got jammed, she blamed my poor friend and told him never to come again. What precipitated her sudden dislike of such a kind man I will never know.

On another occasion my brother, Norman, called on my mother and was surprised to find most of her furniture in the front garden. My mother opened the door, handed Norman her best tea service wrapped in newspaper and announced that this was her parting gift to him as she was off to live with Win, where her wardrobe and clothes had already been taken. The furniture in the front garden – for which my mother had scrimped and saved for so many years – was left there for anyone to take. Somehow Win had persuaded my mother, who had been feeling a bit lonely, to come and live with her. Norman knew nothing about the plan and neither did I, having moved to the Canterbury Diocese, where I had been inducted as Rector of a group of churches on Romney Marsh.

So it was that my mother moved in with Aunty Win and did her every bidding: she did the shopping, fetched her pension from the Post Office and her prescription from the surgery, and performed all manner of other duties. Her sojourn was short-lived. One day, without any warning, Win ordered my mother to leave, saying that she did not want her company any more. Go where? She had given up her home at my aunt's suggestion! Why this sudden change of heart? What had she done? I wish I knew the answers to these questions. My mother had no alternative but to move in with Norman and Doreen.

Poor mother! She never recovered from Win's cruel treatment. She became more nervous than ever, drained of all confidence and very troubled. After a few months with my brother, she came to live with me at the Rectory in Dymchurch. She became a parishioner and a regular church member, first living with me in the Queen Anne house with its sloping floors and low ceilings, and then, when this was sold by the Diocese, in the new rectory which had been built next door to the church.

There is a sequel to this story, again witnessed by my brother. The following Christmas he and Doreen went to see Aunty Win to drop off her Christmas presents, and let her know that they would be spending Christmas Day with Doreen's family that year for a change. On hearing this, my aunt went ballistic: 'I think that yaw are the most terrible people I have ever known, and I don't want to see yaw ever agin. Get out of ma 'ouse.'

To this day my brother has no idea what prompted this outburst, although he had observed a certain coolness in my aunt's demeanour prior to her eruption. Surely it can't just have been that she was displeased at the thought of spending Christmas Day alone! Norman and Doreen never saw Aunty Win again. And neither did my mother. Despite these rifts, Aunty Win still asked me to sort out her tax affairs as she was in trouble and had sacked the accountant who had acted for her husband's business – but that's a story for later in this book.

When I told my mother about Aunty Win's behaviour and how she reacted when she didn't get her own way, her immediate response was, 'Er husband and those two lodgers (Chris's brothers) spoilt 'er rotten. They gave into 'er and 'er could have anything 'er wanted.' Aunty Win was certainly a chip off the old dragon – the old dragon being, of course, my fire-breathing grandmother.

Chapter 10

IN THE NAVY

April 4th, 1941: I remember the day well for three reasons. First, an Atlantic convoy suffered fifty per cent losses from German U-boats; second, it was my fourteenth birthday; and third, it was my first day at work, learning to be a compositor with a jobbing printer.

The hours were 8am to 6pm on weekdays and 8am to 1pm on Saturdays, with thirty minutes for lunch. I'm not sure whether there were tea breaks in those days! The workshop, a former wine merchant's, was situated in a poor quarter of Birmingham beside a disused canal which in the summer gave off a terrible stench. My daily journey by bicycle involved a round trip of twelve miles. On the return journey, I cycled up four hills, one of which – Cape Hill – was a very steep incline indeed. During the war the clocks were not put back the usual hour, so the evenings were very dark, and long. Coupled with the blackout, cycling home became a very dangerous exercise. I had two accidents: on one occasion I rode into the back of a stationary van which had no parking lights and buckled the front fork of my bike. On the second, I collided with some roadworks which were cordoned off by a chain. On both occasions, I hurt myself quite badly and had to travel to work for some weeks by the Midland Red bus.

My wage was a mere 15 shillings per week – 75 pence in present coinage. I gave my mother ten shillings and retained five for myself. The printing firm did not recognise a trade union and so were able to pay lower wages. When my brother returned from the army to work there in 1949, his wages were less than half his former army pay! The conditions were grim too. For most of the time the floors of the composing and machine shops were knee-deep in sheets of inked paper and spoils from the printing presses, so my trousers and shoes were frequently covered in wet, black ink. Furthermore, the terrible noise from the printing presses and the thump-thump of the guillotine cutting the huge reams of paper into appropriate sizes caused the whole building to shake. All in all, it was a very unpleasant environment, but I suppose it was paradise compared to the big factories and furnaces of the Black Country.

The war had taken away the younger men and so a couple of old men were employed to fill the gaps in the work force. I remember them vividly because they were such revolting characters. Both had an enormous chip on their shoulder and showed great hostility towards the owner of the business – one of them even threatened to bring a gun and shoot him. What I found most unpleasant was their personal hygiene: they always seemed to have colds, and instead of using a handkerchief or tissues they blew their noses on scraps of paper and threw the snotty results on the floor. Neither of them lasted very long with the firm.

The boss of the printing business used to organise coach parties to go into the countryside at weekends to assist the farmers with their crops, as part of the drive to 'Dig for Victory'. I was recruited and spent most of my

Sundays in the spring weeding and in the autumn pulling up sugar beet and other vegetables. This was volunteer work so we weren't paid, but we were given cheese sandwiches and drinks on the job. It was the first time that I ever experienced serious backache, something which I was to experience a lot of in later life.

To improve my education, I insisted on having a one-day release from my work at the printers so that I could attend the local technical college. My employer deducted the appropriate fraction from my frugal wage. I also registered for evening classes to improve my English and Maths. I prepared for and passed the preliminary examination of the Chartered Institute of Secretaries. In addition, I sat the examinations of the Royal Society of Arts in subjects like Bookkeeping, Accountancy, Economics and Commercial Law to an advanced level. After spending nine hours at the printing works, cycling six miles home and swallowing a mouthful of supper, I cycled another couple of miles to the night school in Flash Road, Oldbury. This was my routine in term time for the next four years. Ideally, I should have found employment in an office, but I left school without certification of any kind. Furthermore, there were restrictions on moving jobs during the war. Had I left the printers I might have been directed to work in a munitions factory, which would have meant jumping out of the frying pan into the fire.

* * *

Although WWII ended in Europe in May 1945 (VED) and in the Far East in September 1945 (VJD), National Service continued, however, until 1960, with the last conscripts demobilised in 1963. I was due to be called up on my eighteenth birthday, but I was granted an exemption until I had finished my preliminary examinations so that I could train as an accountant after demobilisation. However, I became anxious to get my National Service over and done with. Fed up with my work as a compositor I joined the Royal Navy in December 1945.

I had no choice about which branch of the armed forces I served in. The Navy wanted Sick Berth Attendants (SBAs) to look after sick servicemen returning from abroad, so I became a naval nurse. I did six weeks of 'square bashing' at HMS *Royal Arthur*, Skegness, and then completed my basic seaman's training at HMS *Glendower* in Pwllheli, North Wales. The government had requisitioned these former holiday camps from Billy Butlin for the training of new recruits during the war. Finally, I received some rudimentary medical training at Barrow Gurney Psychiatric Hospital, Somerset, which had also been requisitioned by the government. I understand that in pre-war days the training of naval nurses was nine months –mine was reduced to ten weeks.

Life at these three training camps was grim, particularly during the winter. Living conditions were rough, the discipline harsh, the food barely edible and the training hardly fit for purpose. We were supposed to be budding sailors and yet on the day our swimming abilities were to be assessed the test was cancelled before half of the new conscripts, including myself, had an opportunity to swim a stroke. Although I had learned to swim at school, I knew that there were some amongst us who were unable to swim at all. The seaman's instruction course at HMS *Glendower* was a farce. We had to take a naval cutter out to sea and were expected to row it rather than use a sail, which meant trying to handle the huge oars in a storm. I was nearly pulled overboard when my oar came out of the rowlocks. The morning we went to the firing ranges there was a hard frost, so I could hardly hold the rifle let alone load it. The thing stuck to my hands. Little wonder that the petty officer was so enraged by our performance! It was here that I first experienced Naval discipline; I failed to salute a captain and was put on a charge. At six am I was marched to the parade ground and accompanied by a petty officer and made to pick up the litter. The parade ground was like a skating rink and it was virtually impossible to pick up anything! However, we all passed muster and were drafted to our first posting – in my case to the Royal Naval Hospital in Haslar near Portsmouth. There I was put to work on Zymotics, the old name for an isolation ward, where I helped to nurse sailors who had picked up strange infectious diseases while serving in the Far East.

I found life at Haslar Hospital very unpleasant. For the second time, I was on a charge. I had unwittingly let myself in for what was a punishment for 'neglect of duty'. One of the SBAs on the ward said that he didn't mind doing the early shift and would stand in for me if I wanted a lie-in. I did just that only to discover to my horror that he had failed to turn up at 6 am. I was hauled before the quarter-master and consigned to the kitchen stores for a couple of days. My duties involved taking in dried goods and the like from suppliers; I was so hungry that I couldn't resist helping myself to some of the currants and sultanas I was meant to be storing. My only relief from the Portsmouth barracks where we were billeted was the YMCA in Portsmouth town. In those days, they had record booths where you could go and listen to your own choice of music. I remember to this day playing Sibelius's tone poem, *The Swan of Tuonela,* a melancholy piece based on an epic from Finnish mythology about the death of a sacred swan. In a strange way, I found comfort in its haunting and sorrowful sounds.

* * *

In the autumn of 1946, I was drafted to HMS *Queen*, an escort carrier that had been lent to Britain by the Americans under the Lend-Lease agreement signed in 1941. The ship was making its last voyage to Montreal where she was to be paid off in November 1946 before being returned to the Americans (in 1948 HMS *Queen* was converted into a cargo ship and renamed *Roebiah*). Amongst the passengers were 'GI Brides' – young English women, some with children, going to join American servicemen whom they had married while stationed in England. Our operating theatre also served as a baby delivery unit as we had several births during our passage across the Atlantic. One day, a GI bride fell down a gangway and broke her femur. It was a compound fracture, as the bone came right through the skin. I helped to take the poor woman to the theatre and while there I fainted at the sight of so much blood.

Alex, another SBA who was on duty at the time, was ordered to take me to the sickbay to recover. When I came to in the cradle, he was bending over me and saying something which I did not catch. But our eyes met, and they said something more eloquent than words. Seventy years later I can still remember Alex's eyes, which were deep blue and full of excitement. He was a very handsome man with an aquiline Roman nose, long fine fingers and an athletic body decorated with dark hair but had a light stoop from the shoulders. I had a very poorly developed and hairless body, but an attractive face and a shock of auburn hair.

* * *

The Atlantic crossing was at times rough and I was often seasick – it was an illness from which I constantly suffered throughout my time on board my next posting. During the final days of the voyage, HMS *Queen* entered the Gulf of St. Lawrence and anchored for a night opposite Quebec City, before sailing up to Montreal, the navigational limit at the time. Nowadays ships can bypass the Lachine Rapids and continue to Kingston at the outflow of Lake Ontario. The river transverses the Canadian provinces of Quebec and Ontario and is part of the international boundary between Canada and New York State, USA. After my fainting episode, Alex and I struck up a friendship and spent our free time in conversation. He came from Mansfield, a mining town about fourteen miles east of Nottingham, right in the heart of Sherwood Forest - Robin Hood country. Alex's father practised as an accountant, but Alex was hoping to train in estate management when he was demobbed.

I told him of my humbler roots in the Black Country, my dissatisfaction with my job as a compositor and my aspirations to train as an accountant when I was de-mobbed if I could find someone to take me on as a pupil or clerk. We shared views on all sorts of subjects, with politics assuming prominence, fuelled by our radical views on the social order at home – especially the ine-qualities of life because of poverty and the class divi-sions of society. Religion also came in for an airing and we discovered that we both had Methodist backgrounds. Alex's father had been a Methodist local preacher, and Alex had been a scout leader with a troop attached to his church. I had been a Sunday school teacher and played the piano for the hymns. A rapport grew between us that I had never experienced before – in stark con-trast to many of the crew on the lower decks, whose crude banter was mostly about sexual exploits with the 'birds' ashore, and laced with expletives and sexual in-nuendos, most of which were Double Dutch to me at the time.

Much of our conversation took place on a starboard gangway where we could view the shoreline of the St. Lawrence River. It was 'the Fall', as the Americans call it, and the deciduous trees – maple, oak, plane, ash – were dressed in their gold, brown and purple colours. Evergreens of fir, pine and yew formed a dark-green backcloth – it's no wonder that this area has since be-come the inspiration and hunting ground for a school of Canadian artists. Just as Wordsworth was moved to write his most famous poem when he stumbled upon the sight of a host of golden daffodils in his beloved Lake District, so Alex and I were inspired to write poetry about the glorious scene which was passing before our eyes. It was like a kaleidoscope reflecting the changing colours as we glided smoothly down the St. Lawrence river. Our shared euphoria was not only inspired by the beauty of nature: we were attracted to each other and enjoyed each other's company. Here was someone I could talk to and who was interested in me, something I had never experienced with my father or anyone else for that matter. I became alive. Yes, I was in love. I was free and oblivious to any guilt or shame which society would later impose on me because of 'the love that dare not speak its name' – a line from the poem 'Two Loves' by Lord Alfred Douglas known as 'Bosie', who was a troubled homosexual poet. He had a tempestuous love affair with Oscar Wilde the great poet and playwright who was sent to prison for sexual indecency.

Parting was such sweet sorrow. From Montreal, Alex was sent to New York by train and then drafted to another ship bound for the UK. I was sent to Chicago by train and then boarded the RMS *Aquitania*, a luxury liner turned troop carrier also bound for home. Before we parted, I gave Alex my signet ring as a token of my love for him. The gold-plated signet ring had been given to me by my maternal grandmother for my eighteenth birthday. I don't recall ever being challenged by any of my family as to what had happened to the ring – I do recall, however, a remark made by a fellow SBA who accused Alex and me of committing buggery. I told him that he did not know what he was talking about, and I certainly did not know either. Later in life, I did learn the true meaning of the word 'bugger' when I was in digs in Mansfield. Florence, my landlady, was a kind but rough and ready sort of a woman. She had been a butcher's wife but had left her husband. Florence became rather too fond of me, which often happened I'm afraid. One day she opened her heart to me. Her husband did not want any children and he used to bugger her: this was why they split up. My sexual education had now been immeasurably improved. I learned that anal sex was also practised by married couples and was not the special 'sin' of some homosexuals.

What that SBA had witnessed was Alex in my bunk on our last night aboard ship – a moment of intimacy when Alex and I kissed and hugged. It was my first experience of erotic love with a man and it was wonderful. We did not see each other again for about a year. Our only contact was by letter, but this was made difficult by our various postings by the naval authorities.

* * *

My last posting was to HMS *Lennox*, an Algerine class Fleet Minesweeper with a displacement of 8,800 tons. During the war, it had been awarded numerous battle honours in recognition of its minesweeping operations in the English Channel and the Indian Ocean. In 1944, the ship was adopted by the civil community of Erith, Kent, following a successful 'Warship Week' campaign. In 1946, the ship's company was entertained by the civil authorities and the mayor and corporation accompanied the captain and crew when we sailed up the Thames to the Pool of London to mark the occasion. When I joined the *Lennox*, she had ceased mine-sweeping duties and was deployed with a Fishery Protection squadron in the English Channel, the Irish Sea and off the west coast of Ireland.

I became quite popular because I was a teetotaller at the time and so I gave away my rum ration (one eighth of an imperial pint) at 6 bells in the forenoon watch (11 am). As the only medic amongst the eighty-five souls on board, I earned the nickname 'Doc'. With only ten weeks of medical training and a large medical handbook for reference – plus what I had learned as a St. John's Ambulance cadet – I don't think that I have ever felt so inadequate and apprehensive in all my life!

We spent most of the time at sea trailing the fishing lanes and chasing errant skippers of vessels fishing in prohibited waters. We then accompanied the boats into the nearest port where the skipper was usually fined, and his catch confiscated. The *Lennox* was a small vessel which bobbed around in the sea like a cork. When it was rough it developed a kind of corkscrew motion which made my seasickness an utter misery. It was no comfort to know that England's greatest seafaring hero, Horatio Nelson, suffered the same thing! I would often lash myself to a spar amidships, a position that mitigated the extremes of the ship's motions. Fortunately, I slept in a cradle in the sickbay on the starboard side and so avoided having to sleep below deck in a hammock, which I'm sure I would have found very unpleasant.

Fortunately, my medical knowledge was only really put to the test when one of the stokers complained of stomach pains. I suspected he had an inflamed appendix – a diagnosis which proved to be correct – and insisted that he was taken to a hospital at the next port of call. I also remember being terrified when I had to give the ship's captain some injections — the one thing you don't want to do on a ship is upset the skipper! Ironically, the biggest crisis I encountered onboard the ship was when I developed a condition called 'tetany', whereby I experienced involuntary cramps and contractions of my hands and feet and other parts of my body. I'm not sure what caused this condition. It may have had something to do with my constant seasickness and the consequent dehydration due to lack of fluids and nutrients. At the time we were sailing off the Atlantic coast of Northern Ireland and I had to be taken ashore at Killybegs, the largest fishing port in County Donegal.

Aside from such episodes, my medical duties were mundane – taking temperatures and blood pressure with a sphygmomanometer (a blood pressure monitor in everyday speak), and dishing out painkillers and other medicines. I was, however, kept busy with matters of hygiene and sexually transmitted diseases. *Pediculosis pubis* ('crabs') was all too prevalent amongst the crew: the treatment involved shaving the hair from the armpits and the pubic area and then anointing the bare skin with an evil-looking grey ointment containing permethrin. The subject of sex was never far away, if not in conversations then certainly in the thoughts of what the sailors planned to do when they hit dry land. Every time they went ashore, I used to set up irrigation equipment for washing out their urethras with potassium permanganate as a precaution against infection.

I was aware that there were homosexuals amongst the crew, but it never became an issue (even though it was not officially tolerated in the armed forces until quite recently). There were two or three crew members – one of whom I remember very well, nicknamed 'Loffie', a very tall Leading Seaman – who were regulars at the sickbay. They wanted me to check them out for any sexual disease but this was, of course, a ruse for them to show me their genitals. They probably knew that I was a homosexual, although I never acknowledged it or responded to their innuendos.

Although there was a lot of religious prejudice in my family against Roman Catholics, I had never experienced what it was like to be discriminated against because of my beliefs until I developed tetany. Set ashore at Killybegs, I was taken to a hospital run by Roman Catholic nuns. When they learned that I was a Protestant, a Methodist in fact, they refused to have anything to do with me. They would not even speak to me. They immediately sent for the doctor, a Protestant in the town, to act as a go-between. For a short time, I was put in a ward with an open peat fire and rows of old men who were lying on paillasses on the floor and coughing their guts out. This sad, pathetic sight lives in my memory to this day.

I'm glad to say that my sojourn at Killybegs had a happy ending. News had spread that a British sailor was in town, and when I was well enough, I was inundated with invitations of hospitality both from the Catholic majority and the Protestant minority. They vied with each other for my company, the Catholics taking me to the pub for a drink and the Protestants to their homes for tea! All of them were very friendly and made me feel most welcome.

Later I travelled to Belfast, where for a few days I stayed with some official who had been contacted by the Naval Authorities to look after me until the *Lennox* docked. I remember that he was very hospitable and took me around Belfast to see the sites, but he made no bones about his contempt for Republicans and his pride in being an Ulsterman. I was keenly aware of the religious prejudices between them, but this was the first inkling of the political implications which were to tear the country apart in the '60s and which lasted for thirty years. I eventually re-joined my ship and from there I was demobilised in January 1948. On returning home I learned that my mother was on the brink of travelling to Ireland because the Admiralty had informed her that my condition was at first thought to be quite serious.

My father Thomas Henry Underhill as
a young man before his illness (1928)

My mother Florence Phyllis
Gray at sixteen (1921)

This is a typical view of the industrial landscape of the Black Country from the days when I grew up there.

These are typical substandard houses in which my grandparents lived. They were built during the latter half of the 19th century.

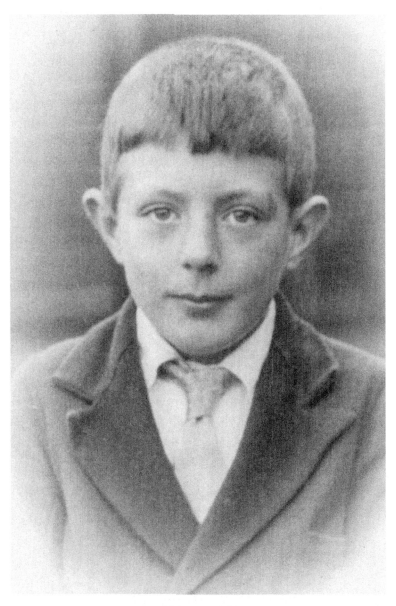

A school photograph
I would be about 10 years old at the time.

My Grandfather Robert Gray after whom I was named.
Sitting pillion is his brother Ernie, Mother's Uncle, who
lodged with my grandfather.

Grandfather Henry Underhill with his
youngest grandson Michael Parr

Aunty Ella and me, aged four, posing for a photograph on a
motorcycle on a day trip to Blackpool. (1931)

Me and other recruits training to be naval nurses
at Barrow Gurney Psychiatric Hospital. (1945)

In the Crow's Nest whilst on board of H.M.S. Queen,
bound for Canada, to be decommissioned after WWII (1946)

HMS Queen returning G.I. brides to be
united with their husbands in America

Minesweeper HMS Lennox visiting the Pool of London (1947)

A flying visit home to see family whilst I was training
to be an accountant in Mansfield. From left to right:
My brother Norman, my mother, Aunt Ella, Doreen,
me acting the goat and my father (1952)

Grandmother Gray taking centre stage on a rare
family outing with some of the family (1955)

Aged 29, whilst living at the YMCA Fulham, London and
working for accountants in Victoria Street (and attending
the Freudian psychiatrist in Harley Street)

Camping on the Island of Arran with
friends from the YMCA (1957)

Me (second from the right) with my partners whilst
attending an accountancy conference (1970)

Between two Brothers after the Clothing Ceremony
at the Franciscan Friary, Hillfield (1976)

Muriel (with whom I lodged whilst training for ordination) with Max, a gay(!) Labrador who took me for walks (1981)

Me, sandwiched between The Rev Campbell Snow, Vicar of St. Edwards, New Addington (where I served my title) and my mother, after being ordained Deacon at Canterbury Cathedral

Conducting a Baptism at All Saints, Burmarsh
when I was Rector of Dymchurch (1990)

My installation as Chaplain in Menorca, with Jim Hawthorne,
Chaplain in Majorca and the Bishop of the Diocese in Europe,
The Right Rev. John Satterthwaite (1992)

Standing beside the Oscar Wilde Memorial, Adelaide Street, London just before I was admitted to Charterhouse in 2003

The Master's Court and Great Hall, Charterhouse
Watercolour by Harold Hookway Cowles (1896-1987)
Painting from the Charterhouse Collection (1974)

A portrait painted from a photograph by Stuart Mumford,
the painter and decorator at Charterhouse at the time

Reception at Charterhouse on my 90th Birthday, flanked by my oldest
friends, James Anderson on the right and Richard Norman on the left

Chapter 11

EXORCISING THE DEMON

I was nearly twenty-one and a civilian again. After saying goodbye to my parents and informing my ex-boss that I would not be returning to my job as a compositor, I moved to Mansfield where I had been offered a job as an accountant's clerk by Alex's father without having to pay a fee for my 'Articles' (usually one hundred guineas or more), which was the usual practice for would-be accountants before the war. Mansfield is a market town about twelve miles north of Nottingham; en route you pass Newstead Abbey, a former Augustinian Priory and the ancestral home of Lord Byron. To the north-east lies Edwinstowe in the heart of Sherwood Forest in Robin Hood country. Mansfield nestles in a pocket in the Maun Valley surrounded by hills. D. H. Lawrence in *Lady Chatterley's Lover* says of it, 'as that once Romantic now utterly disheartening colliery town;' a sentiment which I was to find very true, as you will see as my tale of unhappiness unfolds during my sojourn there of eight years.

I moved in with Alex and his widowed father, and I began work in his town office for the princely sum of £2 a week. I also enrolled as a part-time student in accountancy studies at the technical college in Nottingham and undertook a correspondence course to cover the curriculum of the Chartered Association of Certified Accountants. For a time, life was exciting and fulfilling. I had a job which gave me experience in accountancy and an opportunity to study; and I was able to be with Alex, who continued to be kind and intimate with me as we shared the same bed.

However, it wasn't long before Alex began to reveal another side of his nature, in that he was also interested in young ladies – especially Kate, who worked in his father's office and was a Cub leader at the same church where Alex ran a Scout group. He also flirted with other young ladies he met at the church. I think that he could have charmed the birds out of the trees. When Alex boasted that he had had sexual intercourse with some of his conquests, I could hardly believe my ears. He was turning out to be a real Don Juan. Such revelations caused me utter dismay and confusion.

Living with my boss and his son Alex turned out to be a temporary arrangement and I was urged to find alternative digs. I saw an advertisement in the local newspaper for a boarding house near the centre of the town, so I went to see the landlady. Unfortunately, she had no vacant rooms, but she said she did have 'somewhere' I could sleep. Accordingly, she showed me what she had in mind: lo and behold at the head of the first landing there was an alcove containing a single bed. It was screened by a curtain to offer some privacy from the resident boarders who came and went to and from their bedrooms on the first and second floors of the house. And what, I enquired, was the weekly board for this sumptuous bed chamber? 'Oh, thirty shillings a week,' she breezed. I thanked her and left.

Kate's parents wanted a lodger and so I moved into their house. They were kind to me and I lived with them until the truth dawned upon them that Alex was two-timing their daughter while also making promises to me. Alex was told in no uncertain terms that he must make up his mind to marry Kate or have a boyfriend. Ultimately, Alex came clean and told me that he had decided to marry Kate and that our intimate relationship could not continue. This left me in emotional turmoil – hurt, abandoned and feeling very foolish because Alex's bisexuality was a mystery to me. Later in life I came to understand that sexuality is like a spectrum: at one end there are those who are only attracted to the opposite sex; at the other, there are those who are only attracted to the same sex; and between the two there are those who are attracted to both sexes. Furthermore, sexual orientation is given not chosen, and more a question of nature than nurture. Such variations are found in the animal kingdom, reflecting the infinite variety of God's creation. Alex would not have described himself as a bisexual and my understanding of this orientation came too late to relieve my suffering.

In July 1952 Alex and Kate married and I was their best man, an experience which I found very painful. Fortunately, the wedding date coincided with a holiday I had planned, and I had to leave before the wedding feast. This meant I was spared giving the toast and the best man's speech, which was delivered by Alex's father. I also avoided the possibility of further embarrassment because I was already suspected of seducing Alex from the straight and narrow – a suspicion which exacerbated my own conflicts about my sexuality and my perplexity over Alex's chameleon-like behaviour.

101

* * *

My escape from a very embarrassing situation, however, turned out to be a disaster. I had made friends with a young man who lived next door to Alex and his father. His name was Ralph and we planned to go on a cycling holiday together to the Lake District and to stay in Youth Hostels. Because of the wedding Ralph and I made a late start, and by the time we had cycled as far as Leeds, it was obvious that we were not going to make it to the nearest Youth Hostel before nightfall. Whilst in the navy I became friendly with another SBA whose nickname was Mickey and he happened to live in Leeds. On a previous occasion, since being demobbed, I had entertained him at my digs in Mansfield, so I decided to look him up. I remembered where he lived and asked whether he could put Ralph and I up for the night. Mickey was quite willing, but his father was dead against us kipping down on his sitting room floor. He did however, give us directions to another hostel which was not far away. After a couple of days, Ralph and I crossed the Pennines and were nearing the beautiful Lake District, so we decided to make for Lake Coniston, where the late Donald Campbell had his fatal crash in January 1961. I was cycling at a great speed down Hawkshead Hill to the lake when disaster struck. I'm not sure how it happened but suddenly I found myself being thrust head-first into the roadside hedge and my bicycle lying on the ground with a buckled front wheel. When I came to I was in a sorry state with bleeding knees, a gash over my left eyebrow and gravel rash all over my arms. Mercifully at that moment a car was driving past, and the driver caught sight of my plight.

He stopped and bundled my wreck of a bike into the boot and me into the passenger seat of his car and drove on to catch up with Ralph who, unaware of my accident, had cycled on ahead of me. Seeing that I was in good hands, Ralph decided to continue his holiday alone whilst my 'Good Samaritan' took me to his home where his wife dressed my wounds and gave me supper. Afterwards my new friend, who I discovered was an accountant, took me to the nearest railway station and paid my fare to Birmingham. I spent the rest of my holiday with my parents recovering from my bruises and wounds and repairing my poor bike.

On reflection, even though I was always in trouble, there has always been someone around to take care of me. I had been abandoned by Alex, my friend and erstwhile lover who had married Kate, my cycling holiday had been ruined, and on returning to Mansfield I had to find new digs. I was no longer a welcome lodger in Kate's parents' home after her marriage to Alex.

The Hawkshead incident seemed almost a replay of the parable Jesus told in reply to the question, 'and who is my neighbour?', 'And a certain motorist drove by that way and had compassion on me, took me to his house, bound my wounds and gave me something to eat.' (see Luke Ch. 10 vv. 25-37) The kind accountant from Lake Coniston was the first of many Good Samaritans I was to meet during my life as my reminiscences will show.

* * *

Mrs Woods, a widowed lady who cleaned the offices where I worked, heard that I needed accommodation and offered me a room in her house. She lived in a poor part of the town in a little house in Victoria Street – appropriately named because it was one of those back-to-back houses built in Victorian times for immigrant workers. It was every bit as uncomfortable and inconvenient as the houses in which my grandparents lived, except that it had a bathroom. The front door opened directly onto the street, losing all the precious heat from the house's one coal fire.

The house was very dirty and squalid as was my landlady's dog, Ben, a sheepdog crossed with an Alsatian. I was fond of Ben, but I could not bear the smell of his coat. One day I got him up the stairs to the bathroom and into a bath of water and shampoo. How he loved playing in the water. His antics were so exuberant that I had a bath too! At last, I managed to get him dry and comb his coat, after which he immediately raced down the stairs and into the backyard and started rolling in the dirt. We were right back to where we started. I returned to the bathroom and disconsolately scooped all the hair and muck out of the bath so that it didn't block the drain.

My landlady was very kind to me, but I was soon on the move again because I couldn't stand the squalor any longer. I felt like a fugitive, always moving from house to house. It was very unsettling, disrupting my studies and adding to my misery after losing Alex. Weekly board and lodging in those days cost me thirty shillings (£1.50) out of a wage of £2! It was a real godsend to receive from my mother a postal order for five shillings (25 pence). This was part of the money I had allocated to her out of my Service pay when I was in the Navy. She had saved it for me instead of spending it on herself to make her life more comfortable.

My next landlord was George Stewart. His house was in a little village called Rainworth (pronounced Reneth) about three miles outside Mansfield. A retired miner who had been injured in a pit disaster, he lived with his wife Katherine, a very nervous lady, and a sickly sister named Lizzy. George was recommended to me as a man 'who did not drink'. I did not drink either and I discovered that he and his wife were devout Methodists. George was in fact the society steward at the Methodist Church in the next village called Blidworth (pronounced Blideth). My fortunes seemed to have taken a turn for the better as I was in familiar Methodist territory and seemed to fit in. I soon became involved with their church, teaching in the Sunday school, playing the piano for the hymns and producing the occasional play for social occasions at the church. Back at the house George and Katherine enjoyed my playing hymns on their harmonium, which was in the kitchen-cum-dining room.

In this more settled environment, I was also able to get on with my studies. But my peace did not last. I was constantly worried and puzzled by my inability to feel any attraction to the opposite sex. This was a source of great anxiety and disappointment because there were several eligible young ladies in the church who fancied me but I could never respond in the appropriate way, despite pressures from my landlord and others to do so.

This caused no end of misunderstanding, embarrassment and sometimes tears.

* * *

Methodists take their religion seriously and regulate their lifestyle in obedience to the scriptures, hence the name 'Methodists', which was given to the Wesley Brothers and their friends while at Oxford. Their evangelical preaching was still prominent in the pulpits of the Methodist churches I found in Mansfield and the outlying country districts. On reflection, however, I think that it was their hymns more than the preaching, especially those written by Charles Wesley, which greatly influenced my increasing understanding of the Christian faith. In various ways, both Alex – my friend and first love – and I came under their influence. For my part, my understanding of Christianity – and Christ's humanity, which was highlighted in Dorothy L. Sayers' play The Man Born to be King – was now being challenged in a more radical way. Jesus Christ was not only a good man who cared for all sorts of people and went around doing good things, but also the man who revealed God as the creator and sustainer of the world. In other words, Christ was divine, the divine lover of mankind. My Jesus became not only a friend but the divine friend who asked for my friendship and a personal commitment of faith, devotion and service.

Such a step inevitably altered my perspective on life and lifestyle. Alex came to face these religious questions too, which caused him a great deal of soul-searching. I became his spiritual confidant – the man to whom he confessed his doubts and with whom he argued out his scepticism. To cut a long story short, Alex ultimately came to a similar commitment to Christ and he attributes his conversion to me. Together we joined a small congregation of a little Methodist Chapel not far from the office. It was situated in the back streets of the town away from the two Main Methodist Churches which attracted the townsfolk and well-to-do. Although we were not Methodist 'Accredited Preachers' Alex and I were often asked to speak at the services. Then I started a weekly 'Bible Class' as they are called in Methodist circles and found that the entire congregation attended them. Mansfield had an open market in the main square given to it by King Henry III under a Charter dated 1227, and there was a stall selling religious books. I had already bought Thompson's *The New Chain-Reference Bible*, and to equip me to lead this Bible Class I then bought *The New Bible Commentary* published by The Inter-Varsity Fellowship and *Cruden's Complete Concordance*. I see that the date of purchase in the flyleaf of the latter is 1952 and they still stand today on my bookshelf with their broken spines. Thus, began my life-long love of the scriptures and especially the Gospel according to St. John, which I sought to expound to my friends at the little backstreet Methodist Chapel.

My initiative at the chapel had not gone unnoticed and I was asked to chair a committee that invited all the churches in the town to hear a live broadcast of Billy Graham, a Southern Baptist Minister preaching at the Harringay Stadium, with a sound relay via a telephone line to one of their churches. Despite the Archbishop of Canterbury, the late Doctor Geoffrey Fisher, saying that he was not welcome as many of the churches were very suspicious about American style evangelism, nevertheless Billy Graham came to London in 1954. They need not have worried as Billy Graham had rejected the narrowness of the fundamentalism in which he had been brought up, he was noted for his Ecumenism, he shared a platform with Dr Martin Luther King and had the ear of several U.S. presidents. During the three-month campaign over eight million people went to hear him preach and over thirty-eight thousand people responded to his simple message that 'Jesus loved them'. The Mansfield Baptist Church was one of four hundred other venues in the UK which had a telephone line linkup, again resulting in many people darkening the doors of their chosen church, possibly for the first time. Getting this project off the ground was indeed a huge learning curve for me and was very hard work, especially the training of the counsellors who would help those who had responded to Billy Graham's message. The counsellors would then introduce them to their chosen Church and explain what it meant to be a follower of Jesus. Little did I know that some years later I would be Honorary Treasurer to Christian Teamwork, an organisation in London which had taken very seriously the responsibility of following up those who had responded to Billy Graham's simple call, and who would later assume responsible positions in the Church or be involved in initiatives of social concern and who wanted to register their growing organisations as a charity. More about that anon.

* * *

In the light of my new understanding of the Christian religion and the growing awareness of my homosexuality, my inability to conform to the teachings of the church or comprehend Alex's ambivalent sexual behaviour only served to increase my mental suffering. I began to think that I was a freak of nature, a man with feelings like a woman for another man instead of feelings for a woman like a man – and therefore unable to fit in with ordinary life. What brought this matter to a head was Alex's desire that I should be like him and transfer my affections to a girl, just as he had done with Kate. *Cherchez la femme, pardieu, cherchez la femme*, was his imperative to me. He encouraged me to court a lovely girl named Hettie, a nurse at the local hospital and the daughter of a well-respected man in the town. I liked her very much and she was great fun to be with, but I had no erotic feelings towards her. Alex maintained that I did not know how to woo a girl and that I should give her flowers. I did this, but her immediate response was to grab my genitals and thrust her pubic region into my hand. She then burst into tears and asked for my forgiveness and the Lord's. She said that she regretted what she had done. While I felt a slight stirring, there was no real excitement or sexual arousal on my part. I had to tell the poor girl that I was not in love with her and could not continue our friendship as I could not meet her expectations. More tears from both of us and embarrassment all round.

Like me, Alex had begun reading the scriptures in earnest and had come across Jesus telling his followers that they would be able to cast out demons in His name (Mark 1:34). He then linked this idea with Saint Paul's references to sexual perversions – men behaving like women in sexual matters – as practised in pagan temples (Romans 1:23-27). Without any training, either in biblical scholarship or in medical matters, Alex concluded that I was 'possessed of a demon' and that it needed to be exorcised. Like so many well-meaning Christians he had fallen into the Fundamentalism trap without any regard for biblical scholarship, its literary genre, Christian tradition, philosophy or modern sciences. In so doing, he became exposed to some very dangerous ideas. I did not realise it at the time, but it was this approach to the scriptures that fuelled homophobia in the first place. It became more pervasive as it infiltrated our legal system, became part of the law of the land, and was received as a cultural and social 'truth'. The reason why so many of Britain's former African colonies are at present homophobic is that the early Christian missionaries held this Fundamentalist view of the scriptures. Their present followers have not taken on board modern scholarship or the sciences, and their legal systems still retain the colonial punitive laws against homosexuality. The situation is further complicated by evangelical Christians from the U.S. who are aggressively targeting the continent with their anti-abortion and anti-gay agenda.

The other Biblical text which Fundamentalists love to 'cherry pick' in support of their homophobia is: 'Thou shalt not lie with mankind as with womankind: it is an abomination.' This is found in the Book of Leviticus (c.18 v.22), a book of rules amongst other things about temple worship, the role of the priest, preparation of food and relationships between the sexes, the latter attracting the penalty of death or stoning. They were given to Moses for those who had escaped from the hand of Pharaoh and were designed for their lives during their wanderings in the wilderness and when they settled down in their cities. Their object was to avoid cultic prostitution practised by their pagan neighbours. However, their relevance ended when Jesus summed up the six hundred odd rules in his unique summary of the Law, 'Thou shalt love the Lord thy God with all thy heart and with all thy soul, and with all thy mind and love thy neighbour as thyself.' (Mat. 22 vv. 37.38.) This is now the great imperative for the Christian in our relationships with God, our neighbour and ourselves: to love. In other words, God's revelation throughout the Old Testament is progressive and the coming of Jesus concludes this process and establishes his kingdom of grace and love.

For the rest of his life, Alex assumed the role of a preacher and teacher of this version of Christianity. He became intolerant of any criticism, which he met with contempt and accusations of apostasy. This caused me great sadness and prevented any hope of reconciliation with someone I once held in great affection, particularly as I was instrumental in his becoming a Christian in the first place.

When William Tyndale and Martin Luther translated the Bible from Latin into the language of the people, they hoped that even the ploughboy would be able to read it for himself. It was never their intention to cherry-pick texts and isolate them from their contexts. Rather, they wanted to give people access to the greatest love story in the world, thereby illuminating its great themes such as freedom, justice and compassion. The Gospel writers repeat time and time again through narrative, story and parable that Jesus wanted his followers to 'love God and their neighbours as themselves' (Matthew 22:27; Mark 12:30-33; Luke 10:27) – the golden rule, with no exceptions, whether straight, gay or transgender, or of a different creed or race. In practice, this means treating everyone with respect, courtesy and compassion as you would want to be treated yourself. In stark contrast, Alex became increasingly controversial and dogmatic in his approach to the scriptures and would not entertain any interpretations of the Bible but his own. Consequently, he fell out with the minister of his Methodist Church and other mainstream Christians.

I, on the other hand, took a much more critical approach to the scriptures, delving deeply into Bible commentaries and relishing the nuances of the Greek words underlying the translations. I acquired a copy of Thomas à Kempis' *The Imitation of Christ*, which gave me another perspective on Christianity. I also bought Edwin Sangster's book *Teach Us to Pray*, which fuelled my interest in prayer. I recall praying fervently that God would deliver me from my feelings towards my own sex. In fact, I bargained with God that if He did this, I would devote myself to anything He wished me to do. I made a practice of not looking at young men who crossed my path and kept my eyes only for the girls, but my prayers and pleadings came to nothing. But, of course, I had got it wrong. I was trying to bargain with God instead of accepting that He had made me – a homosexual. It is a common misconception in Christian thinking to make God in our own image rather than the other way around. I sought the advice of my Methodist minister, but although he was kind and understanding and did not condemn me, he confessed that he had no experience of my problem and could not help me.

So confident and insistent was Alex that Jesus would do for me what He did in the days of his flesh, I reluctantly allowed him to invite a group of friends to witness my exorcism. I don't think that I have ever been so embarrassed and humiliated in all my life as Alex explained to the gathered company the reason why he had asked them to come to the church schoolroom on that dismal day in December. Since Alex had come to the faith, he often became very excited when expressing his beliefs and tended to put people off. One of the things which Methodists were noted for was their enthusiasm about their faith and Alex had certainly caught the fire, something which Christians from other persuasions often found embarrassing. Consequently, his prayer as he placed his hands on my head and called on Jesus to command the demon to come out of me and release me from my homosexual feelings would be worthy of any fiery gospel preacher. Well, the miracle did not happen, which Alex attributed to my lack of faith or to the fact that I had resisted the spirit and was therefore apostate. For me the exorcism was the last straw which broke the camel's back: I was plunged into even deeper despair and depression. From then on Alex virtually wrote me off as I was evidently 'beyond the pale' and I was disowned by my friends who knew about the exorcism which soon became common knowledge.

At the Thirteenth Lambeth Conference in 1998, Bishop Chukwuma from Nigeria attempted to exorcise the Rev. Richard Kirker (the former Chief Executive of the Lesbian and Gay Christian Movement) because he was 'killing the church'. The civil response from Richard Kirker to the attempted exorcism was, 'May God bless you sir and deliver you from your prejudice against homosexuality.' In retrospect I wish that I had shown the same courage and wit in my dealings with Alex!

* * *

I realised for the first time the full implications and consequences of my sexual orientation; the censure dished out by ordinary people fuelled by scriptural condemnations filled me with self-loathing and had now been confirmed by my failed exorcism. Furthermore, reading Peter Wildeblood's book *Against the Law*, which had just been published, brought home to me that had my affair with Alex been exposed to the authorities, we could have landed up in prison. All this produced the lethal cocktail which led to my mental breakdown. In the depths of despair, I begged my GP to take me out of circulation as I was no longer fit to live in this world. Fortunately, there were some legal changes taking place at the time about the provision of care for mentally ill patients. In the following January 1955, I was admitted to Saxondale Mental Hospital, Radcliffe-on-Trent – once the county asylum for Nottinghamshire – as a voluntary patient without the legal requirement of being 'committed'.

My experience in the mental hospital was grim, even though such institutions had been through considerable changes for the better since the 1930s. The lowest point was when I found myself in a long queue of patients waiting to have the shock treatment. Most of the patients were long-term and obviously very ill – their forlorn and tortured expressions were pitiful to behold. Some were dribbling down their cheap hospital clothes, which were already stained with whatever they had had for breakfast.

Although I was given a course of drugs which made me feel like a zombie, I do not remember being given an opportunity to talk about my problem – any kind conversation with a therapist was apparently not on their treatment list! The fact that I was troubled about my sexual orientation was never mentioned. I was very upset when they took away the books on psychology that I had brought with me to read, but perhaps there was a cruel wisdom somewhere in this! There was one bright spot, however: the occupational therapy sessions in which we were encouraged to draw or paint whatever came into our minds while a poem was being read aloud to us.

The poem was 'She Walks in Beauty' by Lord Byron.

> She walks in beauty, like the night
> Of cloudless climes and starry skies;
> And all that's best of dark and bright
> Meet in her aspect and her eyes:
> Thus mellow'd to the tender light
> Which heaven to gaudy day denies.

The last verse ends with the words,

> A mind at peace with all below,
> A heart whose love is innocent!

Could any words have been more appropriate to calm my state of mind?

I'm not sure how many ECT treatments I was given, but they had disastrous consequences on my memory: not the recollections of my failed exorcism or of my troubled soul over my sexual orientation, but my technical knowledge of accountancy and taxation which I had been acquiring for the previous seven years. For many months afterwards when I returned to work, I was constantly referring to my text books to refresh my mind on things I had once learnt, and which had been scrubbed from my mind. The best I can say for my spell in Saxondale is that it dampened down my anxiety and restored my confidence enough to return to normal life.

* * *

On leaving the hospital I faced a very difficult situation. My former employer made no attempt to secure my services, even though I had qualified as an accountant before going into hospital. I suspect that he was not prepared to pay the increase in my meagre salary appropriate to a newly qualified man. Also, being in a mental hospital carried a huge stigma in those days, and to some extent still does. Perhaps my former employer was not anxious to make contact because his son's overly zealous activities had precipitated my breakdown in the first place. Whatever the reason, I was on the move

116

again, but I suppose it did make sense not to return to the scene of my unhappy experiences.

Undaunted by his failure to cast out my demon, Alex continued his mission to spread his Fundamentalist version of Christianity with even greater enthusiasm. He brought his wife Kate and her mother to faith in Christ and set up religious meetings in his house, to which he invited all his friends. Later, Alex went to the Third World as a freelance missionary. On his return, he started his own bible school for the training of evangelists for the Pentecostal Church. Finally, he moved to the West Country where he farmed and formed house groups in the locality.

I only saw Alex twice after the failed exorcism. On the first occasion, some twenty years later, I called on him when I was a member of the Society of Francis which I had joined in 1975. On the second occasion, I was invited by Alex and Kate's daughter to be a surprise guest at their sixtieth wedding anniversary celebrations in July 2012. After some hesitation, I accepted the invitation and took the train to Truro and stayed at the hotel where the celebrations were to be held. Later that day I was taken by car by Alex's eldest son to Alex and Kate's home for an evening meal and, of course, to reveal to his parents the surprise guest – me. Kate put on a splendid meal and they talked about themselves for the whole evening until I left at 10 pm to return to the hotel. They regaled me with their stories of how the Lord had led them all their lives, the Bible School, their business ventures, their health, their three children and their families. Not once did they inquire as to what I had been doing for the past fifty-five years or what had happened to my family. It was a very strange experience. I felt ignored and almost invisible: I was simply a presence to listen to their life story, a monologue and no dialogue. As a gay friend of mine once remarked, single men and women have no story to tell!

The evening meal was by no means the worst part of this strange and painful encounter. At the reception, Alex asked me without prior notice to make a toast to him and Kate, but I simply could not find any words to say. It was like I had been struck dumb. I could not *fight* Alex for the hurt he had caused in the past. I could not take *flight* because I was at a function. So, I chose the third option and froze, like a deer caught in the head-lights. It was, without a doubt, the most embarrassing moment of my life.

After my debacle, Kate proceeded to give what I can only describe as a sermon, directed mainly at her children and grandchildren, who were obviously not follow-ing in their footsteps about religion. I thought that it was totally inappropriate to address their friends, a captive audience, in this way on such an occasion. Even after all those years, all the pain and anguish Alex had caused me came flooding back. I was invited to a party at his home after the hotel reception, but I could not go. Instead, I spent the evening alone in my hotel room in sheer terror. After returning to London I was in an ag-ony of mind, and it took several days to get the feelings of embarrassment and humiliation out of my system. I wished I had never gone to Cornwall.

When I came to live at Charterhouse in 2003 Alex began sending me the pamphlets he distributed to his contacts. The contents of these were always a string of texts (cherry picking as it is called) taken from the Bible, but without any explanation as to their context or purpose. Clearly, his views on how to interpret the scriptures had not changed since the time he tried to exorcise my demon. Alex died quite suddenly just after his sixtieth wedding anniversary, and I did not go to the funeral. It is a sad fact of life that some issues and difficulties can never be resolved and sadly there is no redemption on this side of the grave. I bear Alex no ill will and am sad that it was never possible to find some way of confronting him with the harm he did me, but it was not to be. Kate, his widow, still keeps in touch with me and is always solicitous of my health. She was a lovely girl with whom I never had any problems and she never showed any antipathy towards me. I doubt very much whether she was aware of all that Alex got up to when we were young!

Chapter 12

SEARCHING FOR A CURE

Alex's life after my failed exorcism seemed to flourish until the end of his days with an apparently successful Christian ministry and a happy married life in a pleasant part of the country. In contrast, my life held many more challenges and battles to come.

My dilemma concerning what to do after my hospitalisation was resolved by a Good Samaritan named Jean, whom I had met many times at church. She invited me to stay at her home whilst I convalesced. Although Jean was much older than Alex and me, she was one of the ladies who had fallen under Alex's spell before ultimately rebuffing his advances. To my lasting gratitude, she was not at all fussed about what people were saying about me. Her acceptance and hospitality enabled me to wind up my affairs in Mansfield and sell the small bungalow I had bought there.

When I was well enough, I had no option but to return to the Black Country to live with my parents again – the very thought of which brought on a fit of the blues. I got a job with a firm of accountants in Birmingham which paid me a salary more appropriate to my qualifications – about four times my father's annual wage. At least I had accomplished one of my ambitions, but at what cost?

* * *

While living with my parents I was still troubled by my homosexuality, but I now became convinced that I was ill rather than a moral delinquent. How this shift in thinking came about I'm not entirely sure. Before entering the mental hospital, I had been reading books on psychology and sex. Although they were removed by the nurses at the hospital, I had already read something about homosexuality now being thought of as a mental illness. Medical opinion was obviously changing.

Before leaving the hospital, I was given a prescription for a weekly injection of testosterone, the male hormone. Testosterone is manufactured by the testicles and is the hormone responsible for many physical characteristics such as the distribution of hair, sex drive and sexual functions. One of the things I was worried about was the lack of hair on my chest and legs: other young men seemed to have been endowed with this decoration, why not me? I had a great shock of near-auburn hair on my head but, to me, this was not sufficient evidence that I was truly a male. Even when I was given the injections, hair did not grow on my legs or on my chest as I had hoped. My sex drive and sexual inclination showed no change in direction either and my genitals remained stubbornly unresponsive to the opposite sex. In fact, the injections made me more sexually aroused than ever before and consequently increased my sexual frustration. The only relief was masturbation, which in turn increased my sense of guilt as it was still considered a sin by the Church whether you were a homosexual or not.

At least I didn't go blind as some myth-spreaders had warned!

Recently, I read in *The London Review of Books* an account by the critic and novelist Adam Mars-Jones of his 'coming out' to his parents. His father, a Welsh High Court judge, had sent him a letter in which he referred to the remarkable results that had been achieved by using testosterone on homosexuals in medical tests. It turned out, however, that the homosexuals in question were female! No wonder Adam Mars-Jones found this fairly insulting – he certainly might have expected that a High Court judge would get his facts right.

* * *

After a year, the injections were discontinued and in January 1957 I moved to London where I got a job with a firm of chartered accountants at a much larger salary than I had ever earned before. This enabled me to pay Dr Ernest White, a Freudian psychoanalyst whom I consulted in London, in the hope that he could redirect my sexual orientation from homosexual to heterosexual.

I have been wracking my brains to remember who it was that recommended Dr White. While living with my parents I remained a solitary figure, especially as my mother objected to friends coming to the house. I hardly got to know anyone at the small accountancy firm in Birmingham because I spent most of my time out of the office auditing the accounts of businesses in the area. I did get to know the managing director of an engineering firm in Stourport who was interested in people suffering from depression, but I have no recollection of any recommendation from him. Nor did I reveal to him that my homosexuality was the root cause of my depression. My only other real contact was with a family whom I met at the Baptist church where my mother worshipped. I was invited to their home where I discovered that their views on Christianity were very much influenced by a nineteenth century breakaway sect of discontented Anglicans known as the Plymouth Brethren. These Christians had no formal priesthood, no creeds and interpreted the scriptures with the same Fundamentalist zeal as Alex did. I was immediately put on my guard, but they were gentle with me and I appreciated their friendship because I felt so lonely. I suspect now that this family must have provided the link to Dr White, who I later discovered was also a member of the Brethren.

I found cheap digs at a small YMCA in Fulham, next to Walham Green Post Office (Walham Green no longer exists, having been renamed Fulham Broadway in 1952). My attic room at the YMCA had nothing but a skylight for a window and only about a foot between the edge of the bed and the door. As there were no storage cupboards, I had to store all my belongings in my suitcase under the bed; nor was there a table or chair, so I did any reading or writing while sitting on the bed. Breakfast and the main meal were provided, but the residents had to wash up and clean the kitchen after Sunday lunch. If you wanted other meals, you had to buy the food yourself. There was a Bunsen burner on one of the landings and the other residents and I used to boil and fry things there, then take the food back to our rooms. Such rudimentary lodgings were all I could afford because I had to pay Dr White ten guineas per session of fifty minutes every week, for a period I am unable to recall. On fine days I used to walk to work, crossing into World's End and then into Chelsea itself, passing the Royal Hospital for Pensioners on the right, then into Sloane Square and finally to 157 Victoria Street, where the offices of the chartered accountants were located (these offices are now long gone, and the site has been entirely redeveloped).

Friday night was when I saw Dr White. The sessions consisted of talking about anything which came into my head. This technique – called 'free association' – was introduced by Sigmund Freud to allow patients to speak for themselves rather than repeating the ideas of the analyst. In this way, we worked through much of what I have written about in the earlier chapters of this book: the bullying at school; the name-calling and rejection by my father; my over-possessive mother. Dr White asked the occasional question, mostly for clarification. The material I provided supported the Freudian theory that I had become a homosexual because my experiences with my parents had arrested my sexual development. However, Dr White was not only interested in my conscious thoughts and memories, but also in the feelings I had unconsciously repressed through guilt and shame. Working to Freud's blueprint, he maintained that these could only be retrieved by analysing my dreams, which were not subject to censure by the conscious mind.

Dr White asked me to record my dreams as soon as possible after waking up in the morning. Some of the dreams revealed quite a lot about the feelings I had re-pressed because they were unacceptable to my moral sensibilities. I remember one dream I had and its inter-pretation very vividly. The dream focused on King Charles I, who, as I remembered from school, was an arrogant and conceited man who refused to listen to his parliament. Even though no king of England had ever been executed before, Charles lost his head. It was ob-vious that my dream was about my father, who had treated me so badly. Although people don't normally hate their fathers to a point when they want to kill them, these were, in fact, the true feelings I had re-pressed about my father.

When I told Dr White about falling madly in love during my teens with Et, a woman ten years my senior, he sug-gested that this was a belated phase of my sexual jour-ney when I was still mother-fixated, and which thus led me to the choice of a sexual partner who resembled my mother. In tandem with the dream which revealed my desire to kill my father, I had, according to Dr White, exhibited the classic symptoms of the Oedipus Complex, a Freudian theory based on the Theban hero of Greek tragedy who unknowingly slew his father and married his mother.

Although Dr White was a member of the Brethren, I can only recall one instance in our conversations when he made a moral judgement about my behaviour which ap-parently offended his Brethren scruples. Otherwise he remained consistent with his mentor, Sigmund Freud, who regarded God as an illusion based on the infantile need for a powerful father figure. While Freud acknowledged that such an illusion was necessary to restrain violent impulses in early civilisations, he maintained that in the modern world God has been succeeded by reason and science. Consequently, there was no spiritual dimension to Freud's understanding of the human mind – reason and science were the only tools of his profession. Despite the fact that Sigmund Freud is considered to be the father of modern psychology, there are many today who are very critical of some of his theories.

The outcome of my sessions with Dr White was disappointing, to say the least. He simply confirmed that I was a homosexual and that no amount of unravelling of my conscious and unconscious feelings could make my sexual drive flow in another direction. He did not suggest any way forward in terms of accepting myself as I was or that it was perfectly all right to feel as I did. Instead, I was left feeling like Humpty Dumpty, who had suffered a great fall and shattered into pieces, with no king's horses and no king's men to put me together again.

* * *

After the failures of Alex's exorcism, the testosterone injections, and Freudian psychoanalysis, I ceased to look for cures for my homosexuality. I did think about trying aversion therapy, which was still available on the NHS, but when I discovered what this involved, I was so revolted that I dismissed the idea. For homosexuals, aversion therapy involved at its most extreme level such horrors as chemical castration, which Alan Turing, the famous Code Breaker, chose as an alternative to a prison sentence in order to preserve his academic career. He died two years later from cyanide poisoning. Other procedures included electric shocks to the hands and/or genitals and administering nausea-inducing drugs whilst showing homoerotic stimuli.

Although the Roman Catholic Church still performs exorcisms, the guidelines for doing so are now much stricter. In 1992, the World Health Organisation removed homosexuality from its classification as a mental disease. And in 2001 US Surgeon General David Satcher issued a report stating that there was 'no valid scientific evidence that sexual orientation can be changed.' Despite such progress there are still many who simply won't accept medical opinion, not least in America where the Republican party promoted conversion therapy as part of its 2016 platform.

* * *

Although I had abandoned all hope of finding a cure for my homosexuality, I was still unable to accept my 'condition'. I was constantly at war with myself, an internal conflict that fed my reactive depression. My GP prescribed Valium as an anti-depressant, but I soon stopped taking it because it was addictive. He tried other drugs but the side-effects – the feeling of unreality, the dry mouth – were so unpleasant that I discontinued these too.

In my early thirties, I went to St. Thomas' Hospital in London to see Dr William Sargent, who had become a major force in British psychiatry. He prescribed a course of lithium carbonate, accompanied by a strict diet which excluded cheese, coffee and alcohol. Soon my hands began to tremble, and that terrible sense of unreality returned, making it impossible for me to continue. When Prozac came on the market, I tried that too, but it did nothing for me. I now understand that with my type of depression such treatments are only useful for a short time, but much more effective when used to control more serious mental disorders.

* * *

After my experience of Freudian psychotherapy, I resisted talking about my inner life for a very long time. Eventually, however, I started to read books again, mostly recommended to me, and discovered that many Christian theologians were rethinking Christian ethics and defending love between same-sex couples. Instead of portraying God as Judge, meting out punishment for sin, these books were about acceptance, healing and love. The writers had a warmth and lightness of touch – an empathetic understanding of the human condition quite different from the model so often portrayed by Fundamentalist preachers and other catechists. It was as if suddenly these Christian thinkers had found compassion. Even more importantly, their thinking took note of the plethora of reports and surveys by secular psychiatrists, sociologists, scientists and historians about sexuality and human behaviour which entered the public domain after the Kinsey Reports of 1948 and 1953 (even before the Wolfenden Report of 1957).

This new research gave an entirely different perspective to the orthodox views on sexuality gleaned from biblical references. The battle between religion and science, which began in earnest with the publication of Darwin's *On the Origin of Species*, was once again being hotly contested. Over the last fifty years, many theologians and historians from a wide variety of religious traditions have brought about a sea-change in the Church's views on homosexuality. Here are just some of the major players: theologian Norman Pittender and historian Diarmaid MacCullock are Anglicans; theologian and psychologist Jack Dominion was a Roman Catholic; theologian Leslie Weatherhead, the first to examine the religious question through psychological insights, was a Methodist; and Danish theologian Renato Lings, who challenged the accepted interpretation of the story of Sodom and Gomorrah in the Old Testament which Fundamentalist Christians use to condemn homosexuals, is a Quaker. Some of their writings are reflected in the books mentioned in my bibliography.

* * *

In the early '70s I began worshipping at All Saints Church in Margaret Street, central London, where I, at last, felt able to talk about my inner conflict. By adopting many of the new insights about gay sexuality, the clergy had turned traditional pastoral theology upon its head. Instead of homosexuality being regarded as a grave sin demanding repentance, our sexual orientation was to be accepted as God-given. It was the self-hate which was now sinful. God accepts you as you are and loves you unconditionally. Sexual intimacy between members of the same-sex is a gift from God. It deepens that love and strengthens the commitment to each other. Sexual activity without respect and care for the other verges wholly on self-centred lust. This falls far short of the ideal. These rules are, of course, the same for heterosexual people too. The Church of England and the Roman Catholic Church will not marry same-sex couples or bless civil partnerships, although a number of other Christian churches have agreed to do so, such as the Episcopal Church in the USA.

This transformation of attitudes, achieved gradually over the last fifty years, was the catalyst which gave me the confidence to unburden myself of my guilt and self-hate. It helped me come to terms with who I was without being judged. Being able to talk about it to others, to spiritual guides and counsellors, has been the key to keeping me sane and lightening that burden of being a homosexual. For people with my kind of depression, I believe 'talk, talk' is a far better therapy than any kind of anti-depressant drug.

Chapter 13

FLIGHT INSTEAD OF FIGHT

After my failed attempts to find a cure for my homosexuality, I came up with a new strategy for coping with
my problem. I thought if I could change my circumstances, live somewhere else with different people, I
might cope better, so I decided to run away instead of
staying put and accepting my situation. In short, I chose
flight over fight.

* * *

At first, I found life in London rather exciting. I was
challenged by my new job and quickly rose in the hier-
archy to deal with clients' tax affairs rather than pouring over their ledgers, cash books and checking their in-
voices. Freed from my mother's apron strings, I was enjoying making new friends – especially with the students living at the YMCA – and exploring my country's
capital city.

I tried the local Baptist Church in Fulham but found
their kind of Christianity too close to Alex's for comfort,
so I began attending St Paul's, an Anglican church in
Onslow Square. In those days, joining the Anglican
Church meant attending 'confirmation classes', as
Methodism's 'Right Hand of Christian Fellowship' was
not acceptable, although my baptism was. Feeling more
confident about my religious life, I asked the vicar if I
could help in any way. He told me of St. John's, a strug-
gling church in World's End – named after the public

house of that name – a very poor parish at the extreme end of the King's Road, Chelsea. So, I joined the congregation; eventually, I was elected churchwarden, I also became the treasurer and youth leader and served there for three years. The church had been bombed during the war and was now operating from what was called the Parish Rooms, which, I understand, were used as a refuge shelter for ladies of the night in late Victorian times. In my day, gangs still roamed the area and hid their knuckle dusters and gear on the flat roof of one of our buildings. I remember visiting an old lady who lived in one of the Victorian terraced houses near the former pleasure gardens of Cremorne. There was no water supply in the building except on the ground floor, so the poor soul had to carry buckets of water up to her tiny flat on the second floor!

* * *

It was not long, however, before my sexual orientation became troublesome again. Jean, who took me in while I was recovering from my breakdown, moved to London on her own initiative and pursued me unmercifully for the rest of her days. I can't tell you how embarrassing this became. Naturally, I was grateful for her kindness and hospitality during such a difficult time after my hospitalisation, but my gratitude was soon stretched to the limit.

By this time, I had moved from the YMCA and was renting a tiny basement flat in Lots Road in the shadow of the Lots Road Power Station. The flat had recently been vacated by an elderly lady who attended the church where I was churchwarden. The condition of the flat

134

was possibly worse than anything I had seen in the Black Country. The walls were almost black from the fumes of a paraffin stove, which was the only source of heat. The floors were covered with a layer of rotting linoleum which I had to scrape off the tiles with a knife bit by bit. All the tenants in the block shared the same bathroom which was located in the flat immediately above mine. Every time I used it I thought the gas geyser would explode as it made such a terrible noise when firing up. My parents came down from the Black Country to help me clean the place. I remember my father whitewashing the walls of the backyard and the outside (and only) toilet.

It was here that Jean arrived on my doorstep without any warning. I was astonished at her presumption, but I knew exactly what she was up to. I was the object of her affections, and no matter what I said or did, I could not convince her that I could not change and that she would never become Mrs Underhill. Of course, people naturally thought that a wedding was in the wind, which made the situation even more embarrassing.

Jean was obdurate in her pursuit, so I had to come to terms with the fact that she was here to stay. She found a place to live and work nearby and remained in London until her death in 2012. I helped her ultimately to get a job with the Bible Lands Society which supported schools in the Holy Land caring for blind girls, some of whom Jean brought back to the UK for specialist eye treatment. For a time, she managed their Souk in Oxford Street and latterly their shop in Museum Street. Throughout my career as an accountant and later as a priest she trailed me like a camp follower, showering me with gifts and even coming to the Holy Land where I did a tour prior to my ordination.

Of course, Jean knew I was homosexual: she was aware of the exorcism by Alex, my consequent breakdown and my time in the mental hospital. After all, it was she who had offered me refuge when I was convalescing. I suppose she thought – like a lot of well-meaning people – that marriage to a kind and understanding woman could change a man's sexual orientation. It took her a very long time to understand that what she hoped for could not be and in the meantime, it caused me no end of frustration. Her clinging nearly drove me mad, but I had to put up with it because of her kindness when I was at such a low ebb. For that, I will always be grateful.

* * *

While living at the YMCA I got to know many of the other residents, mostly students finishing off their degree courses. Two of them, Gareth and Mark, had girlfriends and I was invited to their weddings. They were delightful couples and I was often a guest at their homes after they left London and bought a place of their own. Their happiness and joy seemed only to increase my own misery and I regretted that I was not like them. How I would have liked to be able to love a girl and marry and set up a home of our own instead of wandering around the world without companionship and a place to settle.

I remember that there was another very intense young man, a devout Christian whom I suspect was a repressed homosexual. I tried to open up a conversation on the subject, but he would have none of it. He was courting a young lady, assured by the Lord that getting married would make all manner of things well. I felt increasingly sad for him because I felt he was heading for a breakdown like mine.

A student named Don, whose father worked for Nestlé and was based in Vevey, one of the pearls of the Swiss Riviera on Lake Geneva, invited me to go home with him to meet his family and have a holiday. This was the first time I had ever been abroad as a civilian and it was a wonderful experience. I have loved Switzerland and France ever since. We hiked in the Savoie Alps for several days, sleeping in the army huts on paillasses. But there was one occasion which made it even more memorable: I took a swim in one of the lakes, but the water was so cold that I got cramp and couldn't move. I clung on to a rock until the rays of the sun revived me and finally managed to make it to the shore by half-swimming, half-floating on my back. I ought to have known better after my swim in the River Severn when I was seventeen and showing off to my girlfriend Et!

The following year I went on holiday with another resident from the YMCA, James D, a Scot who worked as a chemist at the Morgan Crucible Company in Battersea. This time the destination was the Isle of Arran, the largest island in the Firth of Clyde. We flew to Glasgow, met James' teacher friend and took the ferry to Brodick, the main settlement on the island. It rained the whole time we were there, and although we kept trying to camp on the mountainside, we were washed off each time. We dried out enough to go to a *ceilidh* (Gaelic for a 'visit' or 'party'), where we danced all night in our kilts to a lively band and enjoyed Scottish fare. But the very next day, James and his friend headed for home because their boots and equipment had fallen to pieces, leaving me there to fend for myself.

Thus abandoned, I too left the island and stayed in Glasgow for a night or two, feeling very dejected and depressed. I happened to walk through a park near the YMCA where I was staying and got into a conversation with a man about my age who invited me back to his flat. Nicholas was kind and good-looking, and very sympathetic about my disastrous holiday. He wined and dined me and begged me to go to bed with him, but I rebuffed his advances.

I was still uptight about my homosexuality and felt guilty about giving way to my feelings. I don't think that I have ever felt so attracted to a man or experienced such anguish because of restraining my true feelings. I burned to be with him, but I could not. Reluctantly I made my way back to the YMCA as I had to catch the morning flight to London. I have thought often of Nicholas since and wished that I had stayed the night. A fantasy perhaps, but I have always wondered how my life might have changed had we got to know each other. Back in London, I received a *Guide to Scotland* – in colour – from James D, with apologies for deserting me on our washed-out holiday.

My encounter with Nicholas reminds me of another holiday in my late teens when I went to Ilfracombe with a seaman whom I had met in the Navy before I had met Alex. Fred was a lovely fellow who came from Bradford, where he was a server at the cathedral. The fact that he was an Anglican and I was a Methodist prompted many long discussions about our religious affiliations. As well as enjoying the swimming and surfing for which Ilfracombe is famous, we also shared a room in the hotel where we stayed. What marred the holiday for me and no doubt for Fred too was the fact that we could not express our mutual attraction for each other in a physical way because of our religious beliefs. I simply burned with unrequited desire during the whole of the holiday, but we never even gave each other a kiss!

* * *

The vicar of St. John's, the church I attended in World's End, was a devout and caring priest. He was also a buttoned-up gay man terrified of his sexuality. He married a lady who had just returned from missionary work abroad. At the wedding, a very low-key affair, the vicar justified his marriage by saying that it was the 'Will of God', which I found incomprehensible and distasteful — it sounded more like a death sentence than a joyful union. The congregation was stunned. After the ceremony, the other warden and I were standing outside the church for photographs when we noticed a large billboard on the building opposite advertising Courage Beer, with the slogan 'TAKE COURAGE'. My colleague turned to me and said, 'He'll bloody well need it!' We laughed, but it was no laughing matter. Sham marriages are what homosexual men often did – and still do – to hide their true nature and preserve their 'respectability' (and sometimes in the hope that it will cure them of their homosexual inclinations).

Whilst I was churchwarden at St. Johns, I fell madly in love with a handsome young man who was the son of one of our clients. He had left the army and joined the firm, where he was articled to one of the partners with a view to a career in accountancy. For a short time, he lived with me at my flat and came to worship at St. John's Church. Living with someone with whom you have fallen in love, but that can never come to anything is one of the most painful experiences there is. I am reminded of A. E. Housman, one of England's greatest classical scholars and poets, who shared rooms at Oxford with Moses Jackson, a beefy Oxford Blue. Housman was gay and agonised over his unrequited love for his friend Moses, which caused him to fail 'Greats' – presumably his final exams! For ten years he and Moses became clerks in the Patent Office. When Moses left for India, Housman pursued his classical studies independently and published scholarly articles on the ancient poets and writers such as Horace and Sophocles. He gradually acquired such a high reputation that in 1892 he was offered and accepted the professorship of Latin at University College London. However, my lodger's stay with me was short lived as he soon abandoned his accountancy career and went off to theological college, but not before he had taught me to drive the car that I had recently purchased. He soon married and had a family of his own. Many years later I met him again when he came to speak at a clergy conference. He had lost nothing of his charm.

Ever since leaving home just before my twenty-first birthday I had lived in digs or as a lodger or boarder. Now aged thirty-two and two years into my sojourn in London, I was living alone in a tiny basement flat in the World's End. I longed for companionship, but I couldn't have a wife because I was gay and I couldn't have a male lover because my church condemned it and the State said it was a criminal offence. Even to have a male lodger was suspect. So, how could I improve my lot?

In 1962, I was invited to do some voluntary work with a charitable trust called Christian Teamwork, which had offices in the domed section of the Liberal Club near Charing Cross station. This organisation was born after the Billy Graham Crusades and sought to help those who had followed his injunction to follow Christ, something close to my heart when I organised a relay to Mansfield in the mid-50s. They were now running seminars helping Christians to harmonise their religious faith with their personal and working life. For about ten years I wrote up their books of account, prepared their salaries, claimed the income tax back on the covenanted gifts and prepared cash flows and reports. Many emerging charitable organisations sought our advice on legal and financial matters. Among them was the Richmond Fellowship formed by Elly Jansen, who set up a therapeutic community for people recovering from breakdowns. I thought of applying, the attraction being that I would be part of a family. I also considered another organisation called Focalare (an Italian word meaning 'hearth'), which focused on building a family environment with a Christian ethos for people from different backgrounds. The founder, Chiara Lubich, received the Templeton Prize for her work. In the end, I did not join either of these organisations, even though I was invited to do so. Instead, I sought to escape to another country.

The weekly journals, *The Accountant* (published by the Institute of Chartered Accountants) and *Taxation* (published by the Institute of Taxation) were the professional employment bureaux for would-be job seekers in the accountancy world. There was a vacancy with an organisation which supplied the British and American troops stationed in Germany after WWII. They wanted an assistant accountant to work at their headquarters in Westphalia, North-Western Germany. I applied for the post, was interviewed by the head-hunter and offered the position. When I received the papers setting out the terms of my employment, I was horrified to see that they required a full medical history, including any mental problems. I panicked at the thought of having to disclose details of my recent stay in a mental hospital or my sexuality, so reluctantly I withdrew.

* * *

My second attempt at flight was when I applied for an assistant tax inspector's post with the High Commission in Lagos, Nigeria. The British were withdrawing and handing over the administration of their tax system to the Nigerians when they gained independence in the early 1960s. It was a short appointment, but I thought it would be a change and an opportunity to broaden my experience in tax management. That was my rationale anyway!

The late Bruce Reed, founder of Christian Teamwork, realised what I was up to when I announced my imminent departure for Lagos. One day I was writing up the books in preparation for a finance committee meeting when Bruce invited me into his office and asked me a frank and astonishing question: 'What do you really feel about this new job?' My reply was equally frank and astonishing: 'I feel like I am standing on the edge of a mountain ridge and about to jump off into the abyss below.'

The flight versus fight idea got a real airing that day and for the first time, I saw it clearly for what it was – not a fantasy, but a response to a real threat to my life! I had to go cap in hand to Cordings in Piccadilly from whom I had ordered some tropical clothing and cancel my order. They were very understanding about it and made no fuss. Then I had to eat humble pie at the Foreign Office, although I don't recall the reason, I gave for withdrawing my application. Of course, my mother was beside herself with relief, as were many of my friends.

The perception that the other man's grass is always greener is, of course, an illusion. From the view over the fence, a neighbour might appear to have a beautiful wife, perfect children and a successful career, but beneath the surface, there is always a different reality. But in my misery about who I was – or, rather, who I could not be – it was all too easy for me to fall for the illusion of greener grass and allow its brightness to blind me from the truth.

I became haunted by the idea that there was a place, somewhere out there in the wide blue yonder, where I could live in happiness. A place where people were not judgmental or critical. Where I would not have to act a part to fulfil my innate human desire to belong. Where I would not feel guilty for wanting to know a man intimately. Where I would not disappoint women, who thought it was God's will that I should marry them. Where I did not have to pretend to be 'butch' or crazy about football or spend my free time in pubs drinking beer and exchanging sexual innuendos about every woman I saw, like so many of my colleagues did from the office.

Wherever this place was, I wanted to escape to it. But deep down I knew that there was no such place. The problem would always be with me, it was inside me, wherever I went, whatever the circumstances; the one thing I could never do was to take flight from myself.

This state of mind – trapped somewhere between flight and fight – made me wary of making any future changes in my life. I found it hard to know whether a change of direction was a response to a threat, a fantasy of my own making or a genuine impulse to try something new.

* * *

In my mid-forties, I had to face that old dilemma of changing direction yet again when I had to make one of the most important decisions of my life: to leave accountancy and join a religious order. This time, I was convinced that it was for the right reason as the idea of becoming a priest was something which had exercised

144

my mind from my teens and had never left me. As usual, my mother did not agree: 'Yaw werked yaw guts out to be an accountant and now yaw want to give it all up!' Despite her objections and to everybody's astonishment, I did eventually decide to offer myself to God, as related later in this book. But throughout my wanderings before that time, these lines from Francis Thompson's evocative poem 'The Hound of Heaven' resonated with me the most:

I fled Him down the nights and down the days;
I fled Him, down the arches of the years;
I fled Him, down the labyrinthine ways
Of my own mind; and in the moist of tears
I hid from Him, and under running laughter.
Up vistaed hopes I sped;
And shot, precipitated,
Adown Titanic glooms of chasmèd fears,
From those strong Feet that followed, followed after.
But with unhurrying chase,
And unperturbèd pace
Deliberate speed, majestic instancy,
They beat – and a Voice beat
More instant than the feet –
"All things betray thee, who betrayest Me."

Chapter 14

AN ACTOR'S LIFE FOR ME

After I had put my plans for 'flight' to bed for good, life just had to go on. It seemed to me that the only way to survive was to continue to act the part of a straight man, something I had done almost instinctively for most of my life but which I hated doing. This, of course, involved living a double life, keeping my private life quite separate from my business life, weaving deceptions and telling no end of lies. So, I joined the silent minority for real, even though it meant colluding with society's ignorance and prejudices. For centuries acting a part has been the salvation for many homosexuals, enabling them to live in reasonable safety and hopefully avoid arrest and humiliation.

The title of this chapter recalls a sitcom aired on BBC Radio 2 between 1989-1993 – it was about an actor who thinks he is about to make it big time, but never does. I just wanted to make it through one day to the next. While I was drawn to drama and have enjoyed the theatre all my life, I had no real desire to become an actor myself, but I needed at least to convince other people. Pretending to be straight – known as 'passing' – became my strict rule whether I was with my family or friends, at work, at church or at leisure, unless of course someone was privy to my secret, which was rare. Even after the law changed in 1967 after Leo Abse's Sexual Offences Act, 'coming out' was considered unwise and dangerous and was still fuel for scurrilous 'red tops' like the

News of the World. Homosexuals had to wait many years before they could come out safely and were accepted in the community without moral stigma or taint of prejudice. Not until 2001 was there a legal level playing field between gay men and heterosexuals.

For all these reasons, I have lived a double life throughout my long existence, except for the last few years when I have been open to my friends and acquaintances. Pretending to be a straight man has got me into all sorts of difficult and embarrassing situations, which were extremely wearying and stressful (let alone the moral implications of having to tell so many lies to protect myself). The problem that Jean presented me with 'when she singled me out as a potential husband' was only the start of many described in the remaining chapters of this book.

* * *

Whilst 'passing' offered some protection from the suspicions of the straight world, it caused problems when I fell in love with Tony, a homosexual who was also acting as a straight man. Tony was an architect in a practice in Gloucester with another man, who was living from hand to mouth and on the verge of bankruptcy. I had met Tony at a party and fell for him immediately. I was invited to his home where I met his family, but I was sworn to secrecy as Tony had not 'come out' to any member of his family or his business associates. Consequently, our emotional relationship could not be admitted or expressed in any way. A surreptitious good night kiss before going to our separate bedrooms was as far as things went. I was passed off as an accountant advising Tony on his business matters, but his widowed mother made no pretence of her hostility towards me as she was extremely possessive of her son. On my advice, Tony left the partnership where he stood to lose everything if his partner failed to honour his commitments. Tony was seeking a position with a firm of architects in London, so I invited him to stay with me at my flat for a while. During his stay, I became more and more fond of him and thought that I had found the love of my life. But I was in for a rude awakening. At the time, I was trying to establish my own accountancy practice and made many visits to Mansfield where I had gathered a few clients during and after my training. One day I returned from a business trip to find Tony in my bed with a young man whom he had picked up while I was away. I was absolutely gutted and very angry with Tony – obviously because he had brought a stranger into my home and had sex with him in my bed, but mostly because he had abused my trust and hospitality.

It had been fifteen years since I fell in love with Alex and during that time I had not been emotionally involved with another man, except my crush on my lodger from the office. I think that I was frozen emotionally, but somehow meeting Tony had kindled the spark which brought me out of the freezer. Despite my disillusionment and anger with my Church for regarding homosexuals as evil, I still had a sneaking regard for the idea that sexual behaviour should be confined to a relationship where there was genuine affection and trust. How naïve I was: the separation of sex from love was as rampant in the homosexual world as it was in the straight world. Monogamy is the ideal and it is to the great credit of our politicians that gay men and women can now enter civil partnerships, something that the Church should have initiated long ago. Tony landed a position with a go-ahead firm of architects in the West End and prospered. I acted as his accountant until I left the profession in 1976 and we remained friends until he died in 2012. He continued to be a straight man at the office but acted 'like a tart' in his private life, until he found a partner who somehow brought him to his senses and set up home with him. I understand that when he ultimately came out to his mother, she said that she 'wanted to die'! After the Tony experience, I continued to be a straight man at the office but became more adventurous outside of work. For a while, I abandoned my high ideals and occasionally went to bed with a man I fancied. However, these dalliances were short-lived because of the troubles at the office, which I am about to relate, and which ultimately led me to leave accountancy to join a religious order.

I've just read the review of Lord Browne's recent book *The Glass Closet*, in which he describes his life for thirty-eight years when he was the boss of BP and a closet homosexual. I was struck by what he said when he eventually came out – 'I realised what a colossal waste of energy it had been' – referring, of course, to the effort of keeping up of appearances and playing the part of a straight man. He related, for example, that if he was telling colleagues that he'd had some friends around at the weekend, he always had to remember to change their gender and the pronouns otherwise his cover would have been blown. Lord Browne's comment about the waste of energy rings very true with me: to be always on my guard was tiring and often made my depression worse.

In 1970, I overcame one of my fears when a friend and I bought a house in Ealing with a hefty mortgage. James was a homosexual and a Scottish Presbyterian; at first there was some emotional attraction but that did not last. Although we only lived together for a couple of years, we became staunch friends and have remained so until this day. By this time, I had left the firm of accountants in Victoria Street and gone into practice on my own account. I was also still attending the City of London College in Moorgate before it became the City of London Polytechnic in the hope of taking the final examination of the Institute of Taxation. One of the lecturers at the college was quite an expert on taxation, which was becoming extremely complicated at the time and exercising the minds of accountants and financiers more and more. He had left his old firm and began practising on his own. There was also another younger accountant attending the college who ran his own small practice. It seemed a good idea for the three of us to go into partnership and merge our practices, and that is what we did. We signed a lease for offices in Queen Square near to the Children's Hospital in Great Ormond Street. For a while, this seemed like the perfect solution and we got on well with each other.

Not long before the storm broke at the office, I had a brief encounter with the chauffeur of a famous cross-dressing entertainer, but not of the romantic kind! Having worked very late one night at the office in Queen Square, I was driving back to Ealing where I shared the house with James. When I came to the red lights before turning left into Kingsway I did not brake soon enough and bumped the car in front of me – a Rolls-Royce Silver Shadow. When the chauffeur got out of the car and saw the slight scratch he began shouting and dancing up and down with his hands in the air, crying 'He'll go mad! He'll go mad!' 'He', it turned out, was the extravagant female impersonator, Danny La Rue. I was very upset, and my hands were shaking as I gave the driver my details. Fortunately, the police did not appear at the scene. and he went off to pick up Danny La Rue from his club. I never had a wink of sleep that night. The following morning, I rang Danny La Rue's secretary to apologise and say that it was entirely my fault. He said I was not to worry and I never heard another word.

All had ended calmly with Danny La Rue, but back at work things became very tempestuous indeed. One day I was called into the senior partner's office, where our younger partner pointed out some figures he had stumbled upon from the partnership's books of account.

It turned out that the senior partner, who had been living beyond his means for years, was financing his excesses by plundering the clients' account which contained monies belonging to our clients, usually from tax refunds which had been negotiated by us and were waiting to be remitted to the clients. The missing money amounted to several thousands of pounds, exactly how much I can't remember, but enough to scare the pants off anyone. This was theft and a criminal offence.

The monies had to be repaid by *all* the partners as we were now jointly and severally liable for any deficit by law. The only way we could do this was for each of us to put extra money into the business – without this cash injection, we ran the risk of bankruptcy. The obvious solution was for each of the partners to raise money from their respective properties by means of a second mortgage. This was the moment when my cover was blown. I was living with my friend James in the house we had just bought, and he adamantly refused to sign the necessary legal documents involved in increasing our existing mortgage. The cat was out of the bag: the partners immediately jumped to the conclusion that I was 'queer' and living with my lover. I can't begin to tell you the abuse that I had to put up with when the senior partner realised that he had a partner who was a 'queer'. The word 'gay', which originally meant happy and carefree, had not entered our vocabulary, nor for that matter, had the word 'homosexual'. These came into common usage later in the twentieth century.

There was a cruel incident which showed exactly what my partners thought about 'queers', and it still hurts to this day. I can't recall the circumstances which prompted it. I rather think that it was some pre-Christmas drinks with the staff which included an exchange of presents which we opened in front of each other. When it got to my turn, I opened the present from my partners. I remember that it was wrapped up in several layers of paper which took a lot of peeling away before the contents were revealed. It turned out to be a toilet roll! I tried to pass it off as a joke, but it was terribly humiliating and hurtful. It was obvious what they really thought of me: 'shit'.

There is an idiomatic saying 'that you don't really know someone until you live with them', or in the case of the senior partner, work with him. Before we joined forces, I knew him only as a respected lecturer at the City of London College, but he turned out to be a rogue. Before the crisis broke, he gradually revealed the kind of man he was and the reason for his financial difficulties. At first, he took us out for expensive lunches accompanied by wine and finishing up with a double brandy. On one occasion he took us to the Grosvenor Victoria Casino, where he gambled, drank and ogled the ladies performing in the floor show. I was out of my comfort zone to be sure, totally bored and shocked at the profligate waste of money, especially when I learned that his gambling losses ran into many hundreds of pounds. After lunch, the senior partner was not to be disturbed as he was having a siesta, slumped in his chair with his head on the desk. I ought to have known better, what with my strict Methodist upbringing and having signed the pledge. In fact, I never drank alcohol of any kind until I was about thirty. Gambling was out, except for one occasion when I was persuaded to go to the Southwell Races while I was attending the technical college at Nottingham. I remember being brought home in a friend's car with nothing in my pocket. The most irritating thing about the senior partner was that he seemed to have no conscience about his profligate behaviour. He boasted that he was just like many others in the city – having a ball and was showing us innocents abroad how to enjoy life. When we started to monitor the firm's finances and curb some of his extravagances we were accused of plotting behind his back.

* * *

The consequences of this crisis for me were disastrous. I was full of guilt as I had thrown to the wind all those hard lessons I had learnt about thrift and modest living. I was reminded of something my father used to say to me when my brother and I got into trouble: 'Yo, biggan, ought to 'av known betta.' What naivety on my part for going into partnership with such a man! I had been brought up to value every penny and never to waste anything. Stealing money or living beyond one's means were cardinal sins. And yet here I was in business with a supposed professional who stole from our clients. I was very angry and totally disillusioned about where my ambitions had led me. Worst of all, I was now being judged because I was a homosexual and had become the object of a wounding joke. My waking hours were full of recriminations; my sleeping hours were so full of bad dreams that I often woke in terror.

There was no one I could talk to who understood the problems I was facing at the office. I was ashamed of myself and terrified at the possible consequences of my refusal to provide extra capital that meant my partners had rumbled that I was 'queer'. My mind turned to that old device of 'flight'. I remember very clearly the night I planned my suicide. Some years before I had taken a holiday in Devon and Cornwall where I explored the lovely coastal resorts. En route I crossed over the River Tamar via the Tamar suspension bridge; a superb piece of engineering. This, I decided, would be where I ended my life. I'd tell James that I was going on a business trip and would be away for a few days. Then, I would take the car to Plymouth some 200 miles from London, drive to the midpoint of the Tamar Bridge and jump into the river below. I had read somewhere that suicides were more frequent in Devon and Cornwall than in the rest of England and that the Tamar Bridge was the location for many of them. I woke up each day determined to implement my plan, but as the days wore on my courage faded.

Here I was at forty-three, still being bullied and threatened and planning the ultimate act of flight, but I did not have the courage to carry it out. I believe Albert Camus was right when he wrote in *A Happy Death*, 'in the end it needs more courage to live than to kill oneself.' Unable to stand the pressure any longer, I eventually concluded that the only way out of this morass was to leave the partnership and to hell with the consequences. I found a small office just off Berkeley Square and started to practise on my own again. It was the unhappiest period of my life, except for the failed exorcism by Alex and my time in hospital and was only ameliorated by James's stout refusal to sign our home away.

I paid a heavy price for my freedom from the partnership. At regular intervals I received demands for bills which had been incurred while I was a partner, and in all cases I was legally bound to pay a third. This went on for ages. Even when I left accountancy three years later and joined the Society of St. Francis, I was still getting demands to pay outstanding bills. Even costlier, however, was the loss of confidence and consequent depression which plagued me for such a long time to come. Soon after I left the old firm, the younger partner also flew the coop. I can only surmise the reason for this was that the big spender remained impossible to manage.

Chapter 15

GOOD-BYE TO BOWLER HATS

I did not spend very long working for myself before I received an invitation from a partner with a firm of accountants who had offices nearby. We had met at the Grubb Institute of Behavioural Studies, a charity where I had been Honorary Treasurer for many years. So, I joined a well-established firm taking with me my two assistants and my portfolio of clients. For two years the arrangement worked well, and the partners praised my work: it seemed that the sun shone out of my proverbial.

Then, quite suddenly, there was a change of attitude towards me. I was never told the real reason for this, so I can only guess. I had been careful not to reveal my homosexuality, knowing that all the partners belonged to a group of Christians who called themselves the Brethren. I happened to mention to the senior partner that I had met a Dr Ernest White some years ago in a professional capacity, who was also a Brethren - and he said that he knew him and to my surprise made some derogatory remark about him. They were aware, however, that I attended All Saints, Margaret Street, which was an Anglo-Catholic church. This they never challenged, even though I now practised traditions and beliefs which they rejected. The senior partner however, who seemed to be a thoughtful man, quizzed me about certain matters and I responded by giving him a copy of *Christian*, a quarterly journal published by The Institute of Christian Studies, a Christian educational project attached to the church I attended. The journal was edited by A. E. Dyson who had been educated at Pembroke College, Cambridge and who was a University Literary Critic and one of the lecturers at the Institute. He was also a gay rights campaigner before the law was changed in 1967, and one of the groups who formed the Albany Trust – a national counselling agency for gay men. One of the issues of *Christian*, amongst other things, contained an article entitled *Personal Relationships and Sexuality*. I have no doubt that this was the catalyst which let the cat out of the bag and the following incident occurred not long after I had given the senior partner a copy of *Christian*.

I had just returned from a holiday in Assisi and Rome. On the morning I was due back at the office, I had a telephone call from the office manager asking if he could come to see me before I came into work that day. He duly arrived at my flat and told me that there had been some reorganisation of the partners which involved me personally. Firstly, I was asked to share my office with one of the junior partners who was, to say the least, a very unfriendly person and had a personal hygiene problem. He filled the office with an unpleasant odour, but no one had had the courage to tell him about his perspiration problem. Then I was told that instead of looking after the clients whom I had brought with me into the practice, I was to become the office 'problem solver', dealing with difficult cases and looking after those clients who wished to consider how they could, within the law, minimise their tax bills. Finally, it was made clear to me that I would never become a full partner of the firm and would never see the partnership

160

accounts. When I went into the office that day, I found that my clients' files had been gone through; goodness knows what they were looking for! It was like a police raid and I simply could not believe what was happening to me. There was no explanation or reason given for their activities. There were, however, some suggestions that the partners had found some mistakes in my work with which they were not happy. At no stage did they ever confront me with what they were unhappy about and so I was never given an opportunity to explain or defend myself. They acted like judge and jury. These autocratic Christians did not have the guts or courtesy to tell me what had really changed their minds and why they were humiliating me in this way. So, I will never know if their rejection was a professional matter or because of my homosexuality and Catholic tendencies, or if they were using my alleged incompetence as a cover for their religious prejudices. Nevertheless, their behaviour brought back the all-too-familiar emotions of rejection and sense of injustice, anger and humiliation which I had experienced from the partners of the firm I had left three years before. This time, instead of contemplating suicide, their ill-treatment fuelled my secret resolve to leave the profession altogether and join a religious order.

* * *

Alongside their core auditing role over the years, accountants have diversified their practices and become specialists in financial planning, management consultancy and taxation advice. In my early days in the profession questions about tax often arose, particularly with small clients who did not keep very accurate books of account. Accountants found themselves very much the agents of the Inland Revenue in ascertaining the extent to which a client's records had either inadvertently or deliberately concealed the business's true profit. Nowadays the role seems to have been reversed, in that the accountant has become the architect of plans to minimise the amount of tax paid. This practice has grown to such an extent that the line between tax avoidance and tax evasion has become very thin. It has spawned an industry on a vast scale resulting in profits of large companies being moved to tax havens and rich people transferring their wealth into overseas trusts – therefore depriving the government of the taxes necessary to fulfil its legal and moral obligations in providing health care and social welfare for the people. This to me, as a Christian, had become a moral issue with which I did not want to be associated.

But for a while, I went along with their reorganisation of my work and my new role as a sharp shooter. It involved dealing with some of the more difficult issues over the interpretation of the Taxing Statutes and devising schemes for minimising tax liabilities, often in tandem with tax barristers who charged the earth for 'a brief'. In the meantime, I began making enquiries about how I might become a Franciscan Friar. It so happened that the Minister Provincial of the Society of Saint Francis, the late Bishop Michael Fisher, was a guest speaker at All Saints Church, where I was introduced to him. Eventually, he invited me and another aspirant from the same church to join the noviciate of the Society at their mother house at Hillfield in Dorset.

* * *

Looking back on those days, I felt that I was being pulled apart again. I was disenchanted with life at the office where I was obviously a misfit and doing a job for which I had lost the taste. I was driven to face the challenge of altering the course of my life yet again which meant leaving London where I had lived for the last fifteen years, giving up my home and leaving my friends! What had I got myself into yet again? One day, I remember leaving the office without telling anyone and going for a walk to Hyde Park which was not very far away, and then across the Park into Knightsbridge. In those days there was a small intimate cinema called the Minema and, without looking to see what was on, I bought a ticket and escaped into the darkness. The film was called *Love and Pain and the Whole Damn Thing*, starring Maggie Smith and Timothy Bottoms. It was a comedy drama, but more drama than comedy! It must have been made with my state of mind in mind. Briefly, it was story of a troubled young, asthmatic man who had been sent to Spain on a cycling holiday to try and toughen him up and an older, shy woman who was taking a final holiday before her health finally cracked and the cancer took hold. Inevitably they meet and ultimately fall in love. After many adventures in which their love is tested they decided, despite the fact that the beloved was dying, to go on travelling together and follow their hearts! Just as I was about to do in leaving the profession and joining a Religious Order.

When I told the partners that I was going to join a religious order as a first step towards the priesthood they were astonished and perplexed. I should have thought that they would have been relieved to see the back of me. Not a bit of it: instead they invited the sister of one of the founding partners of the firm, a very staunch member of the Brethren who incidentally kept the partnership's books, to come and talk me out of it. She astonished me when she said that my decision to join a religious order was the work of the devil and pleaded with me not to submit to his temptations. This was the first time anyone had articulated the partners' religious prejudices and thus indicated their mindset, which would undoubtedly have had a bearing on their reasons for reorganising my place in their organisation. Nevertheless, perhaps there was a tinge of regret that I had decided to leave and a sense of alarm that I was joining an organisation which, in their view, jeopardised my eternal soul!

A day or two before I left the firm, I met a member of the staff who had been with them for many years who said to me, 'Don't worry Stanley, you are not the first prospective partner to come and go because your face does not fit, but be sure you make them pay for the clients that you are leaving behind, for they have been known to be mean.' At this, my spirits brightened up and it gave me courage to challenge the senior partner about the clients I had brought with me. After some very forthright words from me, the last words the senior partner ever said to me, and I remember them very clearly to this day were, 'I must look after my dear wife, say no more.' I had been with the Society for about three months when I received a cheque for £7,000. It was, of course, a fraction of the potential fees, but what could I do? They never did anything by negotiation; they operated by dictatorship. Shortly afterwards they wrote to me saying that the senior partner had died.

* * *

My decision to leave accountancy, despite my strong dislike of so-called tax avoidance schemes, had nothing to do with the profession for which I had worked so hard to qualify, but had everything to do with the circumstances of my life and the accountancy firm that I joined. Whenever young people ask me about the prospects of training as an accountant, I tell them that accountancy opens all sorts of opportunities both within and outside the profession; and if you seize those opportunities, the world will become your oyster.

Chapter 16

BROTHER STANLEY

My early Christian affiliations were with the Reformed Churches, first with the Methodist Church and later with the Church of England which had rejected the institutions and ceremonies as practised by the Roman Catholic Church, including the monastic tradition. So, what made me change my mind and join a religious order?

During the nineteenth century some theologians at Oxford began to rediscover valuable insights of the Medieval Church, which had been rejected by the reformers, and sought to restore the centrality of the sacraments and the liturgical devotion into the worship of the Church of England. These theologians were part of what became known as the Oxford Movement and their ideas were disseminated by Tracts; a series of ninety pamphlets entitled *Tracts of the Times* and published at Oxford (1833-41): hence, Tractarianism. Churches influenced by these ideas became known as Anglo-Catholic. Men and women also began to re-establish monasteries and convents and adopt the traditional 'Religious Rules of Life' of poverty, chastity and obedience.

Today the Church of England has religious orders following the rules of St. Benedict, St. Dominic, St. Francis of Assisi, and St. Clare, to name but a few. For about five years I worshipped at All Saints Church in central London, which was associated with the Gothic revival of church buildings and the Oxford Movement. As mentioned earlier, this church made homosexuals welcome. Furthermore, at the time, under the directorship of The Right Rev. Michael Marshal, the Institute of Christian Studies was established, and I attended all their lectures for three academic years. It was there that I read a book entitled *The Vision of God* by Kenneth Kirk, once the Bishop of Oxford, which made a great impression on me – especially his emphasis on the sacramental nature of the Church.

* * *

In July 1976, during the hottest summer in England since records began, I arrived at Flowers Farm, Hilfield, the birth-place and headquarters of the Society of Saint Francis. It lay midway between Sherborne and Dorchester in Dorset; a beautiful part of the world. I was one of nine novices. At forty-nine, I was the oldest; the youngest was in his twenties. We came from many parts of the country and, in one case, from Bermuda. As novices we wore black cassocks at first, then graduated to a brown cotton habit complete with a hood and a white rope or girdle; it's one knot indicating that we were in simple vows for five years. We also wore sandals without socks!

Our backgrounds, educations and occupations were as varied as our faces: a teacher, an insurance agent, a journalist, a hairdresser, an office worker and me, an accountant. Some of the novices took religious names – for instance, Roger became John Francis – but I retained my baptismal name: Stanley. We were under the direction of a Brother called the Novice Master. There was also a Guest Master – a Brother who looked after guests who came to stay for a festival or for a retreat – and a Brother Guardian of the House who kept an eye on all of us.

Our days were programmed to include the usual monastic offices: morning prayer was followed by meditation before breakfast; before lunch there was mid-day prayer followed by the Eucharist; evening prayer was followed by supper and Compline before going to bed.

In between services we were allocated domestic chores, such as manning the office, doing the laundry, making bread in the kitchen, or cleaning and maintaining the properties. I spent a lot of my time binding the new Franciscan Office Book (daily prayers), as I was familiar with the art of bookbinding from my job at the printers. I also assisted the tailor in making the Brothers' habits, as my mother had taught me how to use the sewing machine as a boy.

After our initiation at the Mother House, we were sent for three months to St. Mary at the Cross, a monastery in Glasshampton near Worcester, to experience the life of an enclosed monk. There we spent long periods in silence and solitude interspersed by the usual offices and household chores. As I was able to drive a car, I used to go to the wholesale warehouse and abattoir to bring back the necessary supplies. I also worked in the kitchen. Before finally leaving Hilfield for a posting to a smaller house elsewhere we were taken to the school at Hooke, a village not very far away from where Brother Anselm and Brother Christopher looked after boys who had been remanded into care. We were also taken to

HM Prison on the Isle of Portland, which was a young offenders' Institution. A Brother used to spend a week there every year, living in a cell like the young offenders.

* * *

This outline of the structure of our religious life and its duties and privileges tells you little about what it was like to live with a group of men, some with health problems, of different ages, from different occupations, and different church backgrounds (including one Brother from the Salvation Army). While most of us joined the order with the serious intention of experiencing the religious life and with a view to making a lifelong commitment, we still had to come to terms with the reality of our individual natures and characters. There was the overriding challenge of trying to love your Brothers, especially those you did not like or who rubbed you up the wrong way. Some found the jobs we had to do each day boring or difficult, while others found it especially hard to adjust to the monastic life. Living in rather spartan conditions with little time to yourself or for recreation soon exposed what raw and rough material we all were. Of course, we did not have to pretend any more that we were straight as most of us did when in our civil jobs, but we still had to deal with our sexual fantasies and the frustration of celibacy. Although not all the Brothers were gay by any means, many of them were still coming to terms with their homosexuality and like myself experienced bouts of depression. A few Brothers acted provocatively or had affairs and were asked to leave.

But all this was offset by our camaraderie and the bonds we forged through a shared sense of humour and fun, and there was always the odd wise, steady Brother whose shoulder you could cry on. During my time in the Novitiate I don't think I ever laughed so much in all my life. Brother Peter, a Yorkshire man, had a lovely baritone voice and was often the heart and soul of the party. At Christmas, he wrote a sketch about the Mothers' Union (an organisation in the Church of England) which he called 'The Mothers' Onion'. He wrote a song which required its performers to sing and do the can-can to the tune of Offenbach's *Orpheus in the Underworld*. I took part in the sketch, even though I had grown a rather shaggy ginger beard – fortunately we did not have to do the splits or cartwheels! Another Christmas we put on J. B. Priestley's play *When We Are Married*. I played Clara Soppitt and Brother Peter played my husband, Herbert Soppitt. It was great fun.

Religious orders tend to attract people of a somewhat eccentric nature and the Society had several of them. Brother Jacob, who came from South Africa during the Apartheid struggles, was an extremely good cook but took the hump one day and refused to cook. Another Brother volunteered to stand in for him. It was obvious that had never cooked a meal in his life. He proceeded to put the contents of certain tins he found in the kitchen into a pot, added some water, boiled the mixture up and served it for lunch. It looked terrible, it smelt revolting and it tasted even worse! During that blistering summer of '76, the local farmer took pity on us and allowed us to swim in his lake. Some of the Brothers thought it would be a good idea to wash themselves with soap in the shallows, but their ablutions were cut short by the farmer who was not best pleased with them for polluting the water!

* * *

Contrary to popular belief, religious life was very busy and there was little time for relaxation. We were, however, allowed to go on holiday once a year and I was permitted to use some of my savings, which had been frozen when I entered the community. My lifelong friend James and I went to stay with another friend, Patrick, who had left England and made his home in Corsica, the birthplace of Napoleon Bonaparte. After leaving the army, Patrick wanted to live as a naturist and was also sick of the homophobia he had experienced in England. So, like the prodigal son, he took his share of his father's inheritance and moved with Jacques, his French boyfriend, to live in San Nicolao, a small village on the west side of the island not far from the capital Bastia.

Near San Nicolao was Moriani-Plage, one of the largest sandy beaches on the island, which was wonderful for swimming and sunbathing. Early one Sunday morning I went down to this beach and was ambling along the water's edge when I heard the strains of a harmonium being played. As I drew nearer, I realised that a religious service was in progress, but all the worshippers were naked. I somewhat sheepishly approached the organist, a small dumpy, woman, and said '*Bonjour madame, je suis Anglican.*' Joyously she replied in English, 'All who love Jesus are welcome here.' So, I joined in the service and received communion in both kinds from the priest, who was robed in his chasuble while everyone else except me were in their birthday suits.

Our beautiful holiday in sunny Corsica had an unfortunate ending. One day Patrick, James and I went climbing in the mountains and skinny-dipped in a pool fed by a lovely waterfall. After dressing we started to climb again, and I slipped into a crevice and hurt my back. I was taken off to the hospital in Bastia with a suspected petit fracture of one of the vertebrae in my spine. James blamed my Franciscan sandals, which were obviously unsuitable for mountain climbing! I was flown back to the UK and spent a fortnight in Yeovil Hospital before returning to the friary at Hilfield.

* * *

In 1921, an Anglican priest, Father Douglas Downes who read history at Corpus Christi, Oxford and was later trained for the priesthood at Wycliffe College, became very concerned about the number of tramps sleeping rough because of the unemployment and disruption of family life that resulted in the fall-out from WWI. He invited these men to work at Flowers Farm in Hilfield, Dorset, which became a kind of rehabilitation centre. A little later the community merged with a more established religious order founded by Father Algy, but it continued to offer hospitality to the homeless men who were now referred to as 'wayfarers'. Thus, the Society of Saint Francis in England was born.

When I was at Hilfield, one Brother was assigned the duty of looking after the wayfarers. When they first arrived, they were offered a bath and given clean clothes, supper and a bed for the night. If they were ill, they were taken to the doctor and given treatment. Sometimes a wayfarer who was attracted to the Franciscan lifestyle was invited to stay on and work at the friary (one such itinerant, given the responsibility of overseeing the laundry, selected such a high temperature that he shrank a whole load of monastic undergarments to an unwearable size). After bed and breakfast, they would continue their trek down the south coast, hoping to find work on the farms en route. Many of them returned each year and became great friends of the Brothers. Many years later when I was Rector of Dymchurch, there were still men on the coastal road passing through my parish hoping to find casual work. When they knocked on my door, I tried to give them the same care that they would have received at Flowers Farm.

After two years at Hilfield I was sent to live with the Brothers at St Nicholas' Friary in Harbledown, not far from Canterbury. One night, I was awakened by the sound of laughter turning into screams. A wayfarer and a woman – who had left her home in the north and somehow hitched to Canterbury – had been canoodling on the garden bench beneath my window. The wayfarer had tried to take things further with the woman, but she was having none of it, clawing at the man's face with her fingernails until he screamed and fled the scene. The woman was most distressed and so of course we gave her a bed for the night. After breakfast all the Brothers went off to work, leaving me in charge of the house, at which point the woman appeared at the bottom of the stairs stark naked except for a towel around her head. She asked me if she could have a radio so that she could lie in the bath and listen to music. I told her that there was no radio and that she should get back up the stairs and finish her bath. Later, I took the woman to the vicarage to meet Dorothy, the vicar's wife, who managed to get some sense out of her and then arranged for her to return home. It appeared that the poor soul was suffering from schizophrenia.

Another wayfarer, well-known to the Society and a regular visitor to our houses between spells in prison, came to Harbledown to stay for a couple of nights. On the last night of his stay all the Brothers were invited to a function, and so we foolishly left the man alone in the house. When we returned to the friary, we found that our guest had gone and so too had our television, which incidentally had only recently been given to us. When I went to my bedroom, I discovered that some new clothes I had bought in preparation for my leaving the Society were also missing; as was the petty cash kept in the Brother Guardian's bedroom. What a field day our wayfarer had had. Some weeks later we received a letter from him apologising for his various thefts. Apparently, he had been picked up by the police on the M1 with my new clothing and a lot of cash on him; the proceeds of our new TV which he had sold in a public-house!

* * *

As a Brother in the Society of Saint Francis, it was customary to have a spiritual director – someone who kept an eye on you and advised on the problems you encountered in the religious life. My spiritual director was the late John Townroe, who was warden of St. Boniface Missionary College, Warminster, now long since closed.

He was a gifted spiritual guide and I valued his advice very highly. On the first occasion that I went to see him, I stayed with the Community of St. Denys, a missionary order of nuns now engaged in parish work and retreats. The next year, however, their guest room was not available and so the nuns arranged for me to stay with a friend of theirs who lived close by – a widow whose husband had been rector of the local church. She was kind to me and made me very comfortable which, of course, was in great contrast to my simple lifestyle as a Franciscan. In fact, I stayed with her for a night or two each year for three years running. The last visit was the strangest one I had ever experienced. On the night of my arrival my hostess arranged a cocktail party in my honour, where I was introduced to her friends and the local gentry. During the evening, it became apparent that she was presenting me to her friends as a prospective husband! What gave her this idea I cannot imagine because I was a Brother bound by the Society's strict rule of celibacy.

I thought that I would no longer have to worry about pretending to be straight because I was officially 'a celibate'. How naive I was not to recognise the signs, especially after my experience with Jean! I ought to have been more aware of the fantasy she was weaving. On my previous visit she had given me her husband's prayer book; and after the cocktail party she pressed some of her pictures on me, insisting they would be useful when I set up a place of my own. From time to time I had received letters from her which, upon reflection, should have alerted me to her state of mind, but I thought that they were just a sharing of spiritual problems and friendly enquiries. I don't recall on which visit to Warminster I told her that I was considering leaving the Society and that I aspired to the priesthood. It is possible that this knowledge might have precipitated the idea of throwing the cocktail party and bringing matters to a head. It was indeed a very embarrassing situation, but I had no choice but to tell her that I could never marry her or any other woman and reiterate my firm belief that I had never given her any indication or encouragement in this direction. It was particularly painful as she was a kind and godly woman who had welcomed me into her home.

* * *

Some religious orders – contemplatives, for instance, stay put in their monasteries to worship and pray, whereas Franciscans are itinerant and move around the country, thus sharing their life both with the Brothers and with the community. Furthermore, many Franciscans find part-time work to augment the finances of the Society. When I moved to St. Nicholas' Friary in Harbledown, I found part-time work as an assistant chaplain at the Kent and Canterbury Hospital under the leadership of the Rev. Peter Hartfield, a delightful and caring man. For three years I walked the wards talking with and listening to the patients there and also those at the neighbouring geriatric hospital, Nunnery Fields, a former workhouse.

As well as looking after an old Franciscan church situated in the grounds of a market garden, we also worshipped at Canterbury Cathedral where I was invited on one occasion to say the prayers at Evensong and to preach at another. I was in the cathedral one day when I made the next big decision in my life. I was thinking hard about whether I should renew my simple vows – soon to reach their five-year expiration date – or leave the Society and offer myself for ordination. After much thought, I decided to leave and see whether I could pass muster as a suitable candidate for the priesthood in the Church of England. It was a risk, but a risk worth taking because I felt deep down that the life of a friar would not sustain me for the rest of my days.

Although life in the Society of St. Francis was hard, I had learned a great deal and was thankful for the experience. For five years I had not had to fake who I was or face any challenges concerning my sexuality, aside from the incident with my cocktail party woman. For all this and much else besides, I was more than grateful. But for all its potential difficulties, life beyond the friary still beckoned, and I knew in my soul that I needed and wanted to be a part of the world 'out there'.

Chapter 17

THE WRONG MAN

I left the Society of St. Francis in my early fifties without any certainty that I would be accepted as an Ordinand, although the church at that time was short of vocations. I had to return all the clothes and robes that the Society had given to me, and the clothes I'd bought in anticipation of returning to civilian life had also been stolen by the wayfarer who'd come to stay at the friary. So, there I was in my early fifties, without underwear, shirts and accessories, homeless and jobless. It is strange how life seems to repeat itself: once again I was in a similar state to the one, I was in after my breakdown all those years before. I did not want to return to my old profession of accountancy, so I just had to get on with things. Fortunately, I now had access to my savings which had been frozen during my five years as a friar. This meant I had enough to live on during my two-year training period as an Ordinand. After that, all being well, I would be ordained and appointed as a curate to a priest somewhere.

Meanwhile, one big question remained: how was I going to get a roof over my head? The answer came in the form of another Good Samaritan – not Jean from Mansfield this time, but Muriel from Petham.

Muriel was a regular visitor to St. Nicholas' Friary, often bringing us grapefruits for breakfast. She and her husband ran a private school for boys with learning difficulties in the same village of Harbledown near to where St. Nicholas Friary was situated. Muriel's husband had died and she now lived in the small village of Petham some three miles south of Canterbury, but she still attended the church at Harbledown. Knowing that I would be homeless when I left the Franciscans, she invited me to become her lodger, for which I was very grateful.

Having now acquired a base I applied to the Director of Ordinands, attended a selection conference and was accepted for training. After all those years that I'd felt the urge to become a priest but not had the confidence to go forward, the dream was, at last, becoming a reality.

* * *

Throughout my time as a Franciscan it was accepted that those who applied were often gay, but the Church throughout the '70s and '80s was in denial about the issue. The attitude of the bishops was *not* to ask questions, epitomised by the late Archbishop Robert Runcie when he said he did not pry into what went on in other people's bedrooms! Throughout my training and interviews I was never challenged by anyone – neither colleague nor priest nor bishop – as to my sexual orientation, and I continued to behave as if I were a single, straight man, avoiding all gay references and contacts.

So, it was as an outwardly straight man that I applied to the Canterbury School of Ministry to continue the three-year General Ordination course, of which I had already completed one year. This presented no problem, nor did my application for grants to cover tuition fees.

180

The course of study did not involve residence on a campus as lectures were held at the Canterbury Diocesan House. Study weekends, summer schools and training courses were held at the Canterbury Retreat Centre at Broadstairs and Chichester Cathedral, where once there had been a theological college. Retreats were held at an order of Anglican nuns at West Malling in Kent. We also had the use of a well-stocked library belonging to St Augustine's Theological College, which had recently been closed. The Canterbury School of Ministry was set up by the Church to train Ordinands for both the full-time ministry and for people in full-time work who would become non-stipendiary priests assisting the full-time priests in their free time.

I thoroughly enjoyed the lectures, seminars and the challenge of writing essays, as well as the compulsory theses on prescribed subjects which required considerable research and had to be submitted at the end of each term. I also enjoyed the camaraderie of my fellow Ordinands who came from all walks of life and whose ages ranged from the late twenties to the early sixties. As the curriculum did not include philosophy, I took the opportunity to have private tutoring on the subject in order to understand better the writings of St. Paul, who used many thought forms belonging to the Greek philosophers to express his theology. Also, I had singing lessons with David Flood, the sub-organist at Canterbury Cathedral, as I wanted the confidence to sing the sections in the public services usually sung by the priest. Lastly, I took elocution lessons to give me the confidence to project my voice when leading worship.

After two years I successfully completed the ordination course and, on the 30th June 1982, I was ordained a Deacon in the Church of England in Canterbury Cathedral by the late Archbishop Robert Runcie. My mother, my brother Norman and his wife Doreen, James and his brother John from Edinburgh, Muriel and many friends were at the service to support me. By the time my close friends and I got away from the cathedral, there was hardly anything left to eat at the bean-feast hosted by the Franciscans at St. Nicholas' Friary and paid for by James. Nearly everything had been consumed by the brothers and other friends who had arrived earlier!

* * *

During the two years that I was Muriel's lodger our relationship gradually changed to one of close friendship and, ultimately, to something which I seemed helpless to control. In practical matters we got on extremely well, sharing mutual interests like classical music, drama and literature. She typed my essays and corrected my English and we became pillars at the local parish church. Although I paid for my board and lodging, Muriel was much more than my landlady, she was the daughter of a vicar whose parish I understand had been somewhere in the north midlands! She encouraged me in my training and helped me through a difficult turning point in my life, for which I was extremely grateful. But then events took place which shook me to the core and demonstrated quite clearly that Muriel was in love with me, even though I could never respond in the appropriate way. I was the 'wrong man' and I could not give Muriel what she wanted.

I suppose I'd been living with Muriel for about a year when one day there was a knock on the door: it was Muriel's brother and his wife who wanted to talk to me in private. Muriel was out of the house at the time, so I invited them into the study. Muriel had already told me how her brother had tricked her into letting him occupy one of the properties left to her by her late husband before the contracts of sale were exchanged. It later turned out that he did not have a penny to his name as his wife had spent all his money on horses, the love of her life.

The story which he spun about the imminent exchange of contracts was a ruse. But because her brother had three children Muriel refused to take him to court for fraud and trespass, so she let him virtually steal the house from under her nose.

The only other occasion I had met Muriel's brother and his wife was at a church service in a neighbouring village which Muriel and I were visiting as part of my training. They were not regular church-going folk and in retrospect, it was clear that their church attendance that day was to confirm their suspicions that Muriel and I were an item. The purpose of their visit to Muriel's house was to demand from me a promise that I would not marry Muriel. It was obvious that they were terrified that if I did marry Muriel, they would lose their 'cash cow'! Well, I was simply dumbfounded. I did not give them the satisfaction of making such promise and I asked them to leave. I felt like Elizabeth Bennett in *Pride and Prejudice* during her contretemps with Lady

Catherine de Bourgh when she refused to say whether she would accept a proposal of marriage from Mr Darcy!

Of course, Muriel was very upset when I told her about her brother's visit, but I gave no clue as to my sexual orientation or of my feelings towards her, which of course were not as her brother had supposed. Muriel had told me on an earlier occasion that her husband was a homosexual and that her marriage was never consummated. I comforted myself with this fact and felt sure that Muriel would not want to make the same mistake again, but I was wrong: even though she never admitted to any feelings for me and probably suspected I was gay, it was quite clear that she had fallen in love with me.

* * *

After my ordination, I was appointed curate to the vicar of St Edward's Church in New Addington, near Croydon. I don't know how the idea came about but Muriel offered to become my housekeeper when I moved to my first posting. I did toy with the idea and discussed it with my vicar. The small flat offered me did, in fact, have two bedrooms, but when the vicar learned that Muriel had two dogs which she wished to bring with her the idea was quickly dropped – much to Muriel's disappointment and my relief.

Muriel was the third woman who had fallen for me in a big way and I have often pondered long and hard why they were attracted to me, especially as I had for many years such a poor image of myself due to my self-hate. I was incapable of any erotic feeling towards them and it strikes me as odd that they did not pick this up, as I had always believed that women were more intuitive than men. As I got older, I recognised that possibly what they found attractive was the fact that, in my shyness, I treated them with great respect and always listened in a way that made them feel able to unburden themselves. Ever since I could look after myself, I have always tried to dress smartly and now in my old age, when my friends look at photographs of me when I was much younger, they say that I was a handsome man.

After I had left Petham, Muriel seemed to accept that I could not marry her and continued to be my friend. She often came to stay with me in the parishes where I served as curate, team vicar and finally as rector of three parishes on Romney Marsh in Kent. Muriel was a truly Christian lady and it was my good fortune to have known her, despite the anguish and heartbreak we both suffered for one reason or another.

Chapter 18

PRIESTHOOD

I was a deacon for a year and then I was ordained a priest, a process known as 'earning one's title'. Until the 1930s, the area now known as New Addington used to be farmland and woodland in the southeast of the ancient parish of Addington. In 1807 Addington Palace, an eighteenth-century mansion, became the second home for six successive Archbishops of Canterbury. Later, it housed the Royal School of Church Music where I used to celebrate Holy Communion. In the '30s, to ease overcrowding in the slums of south London and Croydon, the area was developed with the intention of creating a 'garden village' including houses, shops, churches and cinemas. The war prevented further development until 1968 when blocks of high-rise flats and houses were built for the new generation of people leaving overcrowded London.

In the '70s, New Addington became an area of social deprivation with poor standards of health and education and a reputation for gang violence and anti-social behaviour. This was certainly true during my time at St. Edwards. One of my first duties early on Sunday mornings was to clean the church door after it had been decorated with graffiti and condoms the night before. On two occasions as I was rushing off to the cemetery to take a funeral, I discovered that the petrol had been siphoned from my Citroën car. The entrance to the new swimming pool was made of glass and had been cracked, and the small shopping centre was always knee-deep in rubbish. Some of the more frightening acts of vandalism included shoving lighted paper through the letterboxes of flats sometimes occupied by elderly people and damaging the lifts in the high-rise blocks, marooning tenants on the top floors and causing mayhem. The fire brigade never had a moment's peace.

* * *

One day I was out shopping in a nearby mall when I was approached by a Nigerian sporting impressive dreadlocks. He wished to speak to me, so I somewhat hesitantly invited him back to my small flat in the complex opposite the church. He explained that his wife had left him and their three children, two girls and a young boy. He was extremely angry as the social services were trying to separate him from his children and take them into care. As far as I could gather, he was inflicting army discipline on them and they were afraid of him. I had no idea whether he had any religious leanings and I was at a loss as to how I could diffuse his anger and frustration. After I had listened to his story, he asked me about my religion and I told him that I believed in a God of Love. At this he exploded with such incandescent rage I thought my time had come. Fortunately, he calmed down and together we began to build a relationship of trust and friendship.

He visited me on many occasions and gradually, through our conversations, his aggression subsided. I was able to represent him in court when the custody order was about to be enforced. I spoke forcibly in his defence and the order was dropped. My Nigerian family's first appearance in church was a bit of a shock – especially the dreadlocks – but soon the members of the congregation took them to their hearts. I am proud to say that he and his children were later confirmed by the late Archbishop Robert Runcie.

Equally rewarding was my work with the local youth club, a thriving group with an enterprising programme. We put on a couple of stage productions which I wrote and directed. We visited a TV studio to improve our production techniques. We went on a retreat where, amongst other things, we made the special bread and the vestments for the service of Holy Communion which the vicar took when he came to visit us on Sunday.

Of course, these happy rhythms of community life received a jolt now and again. One day I was asked to go and visit one of our parishioners, a patient at the Mayday University Hospital in Croydon. He was an elderly man who was very ill and told me that he thought he was dying, and he asked me to stay with him. Somehow I could not bring myself to do so, even though he clung to me. He was a good man and a faithful worshipper, and as a priest I should have been there to give him comfort and assurance of God's love and that death was not the end. I was ashamed of myself for neglecting that sacred duty and privilege of allaying his fears and anxieties at the end of his life. He died a few days later and I have always felt that I had failed him.

On a lighter note I remember being asked by the rector to take a service of the internment of ashes in our churchyard. The rector rushed off to his weekend duties as a chaplain to an army cadet unit but without indicating where the urn, containing the ashes, was kept. Fortunately, the churchwarden spotted an urn on top of the wardrobe for the choir robes. The relatives of the deceased arrived, and the prayers were said, and the ashes were with due ceremony emptied into the ground. When the rector returned from camp he produced the correct urn which was in his study at the rectory – the ashes which I had interred belonged to someone whose relatives had not turned up! It was winter, but I got up very early the very next morning and dressed in over-coat and wellingtons and buried the correct ashes with those of the man whose relatives had deserted him. I felt like one of those nineteenth-century body snatchers only in reverse.

* * *

In the 1980s the BBC broadcast live Sunday morning services from churches up and down the country. One Sunday they came to St. Edwards in New Addington and, on that occasion, I was asked to preach. It was Easter Sunday, and, in my sermon, I referred to the Venerable Bede's account of King Oswald of Northumbria's conversion to Christianity through the preaching on the Resurrection of Christ. When I returned to my flat after the service, I received a phone call from a lady whom I had not spoken to since I trained as an account-ant in Nottinghamshire some thirty years previously. She was suspicious of mainstream Christians because she said they did not take the Bible seriously enough, but she congratulated me on my sermon that morning and my references to the scriptures. Well, I was glad that she regarded my preaching as kosher, so to speak, but also astonished that she had contacted me after so long. In my twenties, I used to worship with a group of Fundamentalist Christians in which she was a leading light, but after my failed exorcism, breakdown and hospitalisation I never saw or heard from any of them again. So much for their Christian charity and fellowship. That Sunday morning, however, I seemed to have redeemed myself.

Throughout my time in the ministry, I kept my homosexuality under wraps but there were many times when I was intensely aware of my loneliness and need for intimacy. Of course, this just had to be endured, as did my periodic depressions. Oddly, living amid many kind people with whom I came into contact every day seemed to exacerbate my own need for companionship.

Towards the end of my curacy at St. Edwards, a bishop in New Zealand asked the rector if he would take on a young priest, Kerry, who required what he called 'discipline'. Kerry was in his mid-twenties when he came to us and my what a charmer he was. For a while, he shared my flat. 'G'day' was his laidback greeting to the congregation, in true Kiwi fashion. He was an extremely good communicator and had a winning way with almost everyone. I fell for him, but he turned out to be a ladykiller. After I left New Addington I heard that a very irate churchwarden had appeared on the rector's doorstep, ranting 'Your bloody curate has run off with my wife!' Kerry had indeed eloped with the poor man's wife and returned to New Zealand with her.

* * *

Although it was customary to remain a curate for three years, after two years at St. Edwards the Bishop of Croydon felt that I should make a move to a more responsible position. Accordingly, I applied for a vacancy in the Cannock Team to be responsible for St. Aiden's Church, Cannock, in the Diocese of Lichfield – not far from the M6 and within easy reach of my hometown of Oldbury, where my mother and brother still lived. After the closure of Cannock Colliery in 1967 there was a general decline of industry and consequently considerable unemployment. Even when I arrived in the 80s, there was still an air of hopelessness and depression. My churchwarden could not find a job. Despite his antipathy to learning a new skill, I encouraged him to operate a computer and found someone to give him a second chance. I was soon made aware of the socialist ambience of the place when I horrified the barman by suggesting we might have wine as well as beer at a social event! However, we soon put our inverted snobberies aside and I became a regular visitor at the local miners' welfare club just around the corner from St. Aiden's. The Bishop of Wolverhampton once likened the church to a cinema because it had a sloping floor, an unusual feature created to avoid the potential subsidence that could have resulted from being built above an old mine shaft. The church was opened in July 1956 and was paid for by house-to-house collections from the people in the area. In July 1986 I was there when the church celebrated its thirtieth anniversary with special services, events and exhibitions. I still have one of the handsome commemorative china mugs we had made to mark the occasion. One of the opportunities I enjoyed whilst at St. Aiden's

192

was being invited to talk to the children at the local Junior School during their morning assemblies. Normally a daunting challenge in the art of communication for any priest, but I found it surprisingly easy to establish a dialogue. It said a lot for their teachers.

* * *

Every year I held classes for people who wanted to be confirmed. I also invited those who wished to deepen their commitment to Christ and to explore afresh religious doctrines and the teachings of the church. A lady who was on the fringe of church life started coming to these sessions and soon challenged much of what was being said. It was clear that she had a problem, so we met to talk many times. It transpired that she had been abused by her father when she was a girl. She had never received any counselling and so the trauma had festered inside her for years. Somehow, she had managed to get married and have two children whom she loved, but she had never revealed her problem to anyone. Understandably, she could not forgive her father or come to terms with what had happened.

As she talked more about her secret, I realised that I was in some way exceeding my brief as I was not a social worker. On reflection, however, it seemed to me that her problem at heart was more in the realm of the spiritual than the psychological. She wanted to be accepted. She wanted to be able to forgive her father but could not do so in her present frame of mind. We wrestled with the relevant issues in terms of my understanding of Jesus' command to love ourselves; the belief that God accepts us as we are, warts, wounds and all; and the principle that healing and reconciliation can only come through forgiveness (letting go) and acceptance. These, of course, were all things that I had had to learn myself over the years to overcome my own self-hatred because I was born a homosexual. I helped her to come to terms with what had happened, and she later became a moving spirit in the church, forming and leading a group to help other women who had suffered in the same way as she had done. Every year since I left Cannock not only did she send me Christmas greetings, but a postcard from Taizé where she and her family took an annual retreat. Whilst I was at Cannock, I too had visited Taizé, near Cluny in the south of France; an ecumenical retreat centre especially for young people. It is run by an order of Brothers who come from many different countries and Christian denominations. I was so impressed with their witness, worship, singing and their integrity and especially because all Christian labels were abandoned that I have recommended the place wherever I have served.

* * *

Before leaving Cannock for pastures new I can't resist relating two incidents which highlighted how difficult it is for a culture to change. As a way of presenting the sermon one Sunday, I wrote a playlet based on the 'Parable of the Workers in the Vineyard' that Jesus told to illustrate what the Kingdom of Heaven was like (Matt. 20 vs. 1-16). I invited members of the congregation to take the different parts. The punch line which caused an uproar was when the owner of the vineyard paid the labourer who had worked in the vineyard only for an hour the same amount of money as that paid to the labourer who had toiled all day. One of the players, whose husband was a member of a Trade Union, protested and said that the treatment of the labourer was unfair. I pointed out that the owner of the vineyard did nothing wrong as he paid the labourers the amount he had promised them. This did not satisfy her. Then I pointed out that it was not the fault of the labourer who only had the opportunity to work for an hour as he too had a wife and family to care for just like the men who had worked all day. No, it's not right, she continued, the workers would call a strike to force the owner to address the inequity! Despite the protest that the parable had caused I think the congregation got the point. Whilst writing about this reminiscence I was reminded of a line of an old hymn I used to know as young man, here it is: 'For the love of God is broader than the measure of man's mind; and the heart of the Eternal is wonderfully kind.' Words by Frederick Faber in 1854.

The Church of England had been in turmoil for some time over whether women should be ordained to the priesthood. However, in 1994 Pamela Freeman was ordained deacon and was attached to my church St. Aiden's, but was under the direct supervision of the team rector the Rev. John Linford who incidentally reprimanded me for inviting the Bishop of Lichfield to one our special services celebrating our thirtieth anniversary without his knowledge! I personally had no problem with women as deacons. All my life I had been a fan of Elsie Chamberlin, a Congregationalist who was the first woman chaplain to the armed forces and a broadcaster, and the Methodist, Pauline Webb who became the Vice Moderator of the World Council of Churches and Vice President of the Methodist Conference; they were both inspirational and gifted leaders in the church. In the Gospels Jesus accepted women on the same terms as men in defiance of the prevailing culture where men dominated all things. In fact, it was a woman, Mary Magdalene, who brought the news of the risen Christ to the disciples who thought that she had gone mad. I will never understand why the early church stuck with male dominance after the example of Jesus! My view, however, was not shared by some members of the congregation, especially my servers. The question arose as to where Pamela should sit in the sanctuary. The head server refused to give up his seat, so I said that she could have mine! Ultimately, they relented and gradually she was accepted but not until Pamela had taken her grievances to Christopher Mayfield the then Bishop of Wolverhampton. I understand, however, that many women had a hard time of it in the early years even in some of our cathedrals! Not long after this incident we had a visit from the Bishop of the Diocese, the late Keith Sutton, and I related to him the problem I had experienced. I remember him saying to me, 'Well done you.' He was well experienced in conflict as he had been the Archbishop's envoy to support Archbishop Desmond Tutu in the apartheid-torn South Africa in the 1980s.

A couple of funny recollections before I move on. I prepared a young couple for marriage. They were very much in love and it was a joy to meet them. However, the wedding day arrived, and I greeted the bride at the door of the church but to my astonishment, she was not wearing the usual flowing white gown, but she was in redskins, her hair had been braided and no stockings – just sandals. The nearest I could place the fashion would be the dress of a squaw belonging to a North American indigenous tribe. However, I led her down the aisle to her intended waiting at the altar, who, to my amazement, had had his head shaved leaving only a strip of hair down the middle of the head which had been dyed green and then plastered with styling gel so that it stood upright on top of his head. I understand that it was called 'Mohican hairstyle'. The rest of his clothing and that of his best man was an assortment of garments that I failed to recognise but was told afterwards that it was what was called 'punk fashion' taken from some of Vivienne Westwood designs! After the shock of the unusual, *de rigueur* of the bridal couple, the ceremony proceeded without further distraction and my punk couple went off to the wedding feast at the local pub. I don't know if they feasted on deer steaks and mushrooms and infusions from berries and twigs. I was not invited!

One last reminiscence; I don't remember whose funeral it was, but I remember very clearly one of the late mourners. I was sitting beside the Funeral Director in the hearse waiting outside the church. He suddenly turned to me and said, 'Stanley look to your left and see who's walking up the path to the church'. So, I turned and there was an unaccompanied woman dressed in a black Lycra catsuit and black patent leather high heeled shoes. Without going into detail, it is sufficient to say that there was little of her left to the imagination! As I led the coffin and bearers into the church, I caught a glimpse of the lady hiding in the back seat. I have often wondered who she was!

Throughout my ministry in Cannock I kept my homosexuality under wraps, although for a time I enjoyed the friendship of another team vicar based at a nearby church, St. Chads, who knew I was gay and accepted me for who I was. When he married, my loneliness made itself felt again. Sadly, this very caring priest died of a brain tumour not long after I had left Cannock.

* * *

After three years at St. Aiden's I was headhunted by the Canterbury Diocese and invited to become Rector of the Benefice of three churches on Romney Marsh in Kent. Dymchurch on Romney Marsh was not unknown to me as I had made a couple of visits there while living with Muriel in Petham, near Canterbury.

Situated on the Kent coast between Rye to the west and Folkestone to the east, Dymchurch bay has lovely sandy beaches and is a popular seaside resort attracting many holiday-makers during the summer months. It is also famous for the Romney, Hythe and Dymchurch railway which runs between Hythe in the east and Dungeness in the west. Originally drained by the Romans, the land is low-lying and in recent years the sea defences have had to be extended and strengthened to prevent flooding. The soil is rich and for many years supported sheep farming, with 'marsh lamb' exported as far afield as Argentina. Nowadays the land has largely been given over to horticulture with a multitude of greenhouses and cloches producing all manner of soft fruits.

There are seventeen medieval churches on the marsh, but I was responsible for three of them. The main church was SS. Peter and Paul in Dymchurch, a Norman church built in about 1150 AD. I was also responsible for SS. Peter and Paul in Newchurch which appears to have existed since the mid-900s and was built by monks from Canterbury who farmed the adjoining land. Finally, All Saints in Burmarsh which was also built by the monks from Canterbury, possibly on the site of an Anglo-Saxon church after the Norman Conquest.

My rectory in Dymchurch was a Queen Anne house with sloping bedroom floors, a walnut tree in the back garden and a horse-mounting stone at the side of the front garden. Enid Blyton of *Noddy* fame stayed there in 1945 to write *Five Go to Smuggler's Top*. The Diocese sold the rectory during my incumbency and it is now a guest house offering bed and breakfast. I moved into a modern house on a site adjoining the church and lived there for about four years. One of my first visitors to the new rectory was the late Archbishop Robert Runcie. Canterbury was only twenty miles away and his chaplain would drive him to Dymchurch for a swim in the lovely bay, where he hoped he would not be recognised. He used the rectory as a changing room on several occasions.

Dymchurch was a fascinating place. Cut off from the rest of Kent during the eighteenth and nineteenth centuries, it was renowned for its smuggling of brandy and tobacco as popularised in the *Doctor Syn* stories written by Russell Thorndike, an actor who lived in the village in the early 1900s. Coincidentally, some months before I knew of the vacancy in Dymchurch I had purchased the six *Doctor Syn* books from a second-hand bookshop and taken them on holiday to read. Now here I was, the Rector of Dymchurch, following in the footsteps of the Reverend Doctor Christopher Syn; a country parson by day, smuggler by night! Every other year the community reenacted the highlights of Thorndike's books at a festival, and twice I played Doctor Syn. It was great fun, but I had a stand-in for the masked horseman known as 'The Scarecrow,' whose alias was the parsimonious parson who terrorised the local villagers. I found the people very friendly and they were very kind to me and my widowed mother who lived with me some of the time.

Undue attention from single or widowed ladies, who usually outnumber the men in a congregation, is a well-known hazard for a bachelor priest. I was approaching sixty when I was inducted as rector of this trio of churches, so I really thought that the likelihood of my being a target of female attention would be remote. Not a bit of it. I was warned about a young woman in the choir who for some reason was very unhappy and would sooner or later find some way of getting my attention. And so she did; she told me that she was depressed and asked if she could come and talk to me. She certainly struck a chord with me because of my long struggle with depression, and I invited her to come to the rectory many times. Getting on for thirty, she was a very intelligent and sensitive woman and an excellent photographer who also wrote poetry. She had no confidence in herself and could not hold down a job, so she spent much of her time with an organisation called Rainbow which provided group therapy for people experiencing personal difficulties.

She had a troubled relationship with her father and was very angry with him. I found it difficult to understand this as he seemed to be a mild, inoffensive man who would not hurt anyone, whereas his wife was the more dominant partner. Of course, the inevitable happened. I was single and unattached, so why could I not marry her? I was still in the closet and could not tell her that I was homosexual, and with this crucial omission anything else I said to counter the idea of marriage only made her angry and more depressed. One day the rectory doorbell rang and Dulcie, one of the ladies from the church and the salt of the earth, said to me 'Stanley, have you seen what's written on your wall?' 'No, I haven't,' I replied. Accompanied by my mother, who was living with me at the time, I went outside to inspect. Whitewashed in huge, bold letters on the rectory wall for all to see was the famous line from *Hamlet*: 'To be, or not to be, that is the question.' And there, sitting on the garden wall was the young woman, very distressed and crying bitterly. I did my best to comfort her and after some time Dulcie was able to take her home. Sadly, she had to go away from the parish for a while to have some treatment. When she eventually returned, she was much more stable and in time was able to hold a job down. She became the church's resident photographer and to this day my drawers are full of her photo albums and records of church events until 1992 when I left Dymchurch to establish the first full-time chaplaincy on the island of Menorca. I have had Christmas cards from her every year since my retirement. She found herself a boyfriend and they have lived happily together for many years.

* * *

In 1992 towards the end of my time at Dymchurch the gay issue was becoming more public in the Church and was the subject of heated debates in the Synod, which are continuing even at the time of finishing this book in 2018. I remained silent on the subject, especially when I discovered that some of my church members were homophobic. I inherited a lay reader – a layperson who assisted the priest and is trained to preach. I found to be somewhat awkward and hostile. After leaving the probation service, he tried his hand with a firm of solicitors but that did not work out and he became unemployed. He wanted to go forward as an Ordinand for the Local Ordained Ministry, a new scheme which the Diocese of Canterbury was initiating because of the shortage of cash and clergy. I allowed him to go forward but the final decision lay with the Parochial Church Council, who by a large majority at a special meeting turned him down. He blamed me for the outcome and threatened to expose my homosexuality, although as far as I was aware he had no evidence, only his own suspicions. I refused to 'review my position' as he put it. Given the continued hypocrisy of the church authorities, I was not prepared to come out of the closet. He remained a thorn in my flesh and continued to spread his bitter disappointment to others.

This incident brought home to me the downside of hiding my homosexuality: it could be used as a weapon for blackmail. But it also inhibited me from helping other

202

people in my congregations who were hiding their sexuality, as any attempt to do so would have exposed mine.

* * *

As far as I know, there are no rules for clergymen about taking time off from the parish. I was not an employee of the church but a freeholder and in one sense my own boss. In any case, you certainly could not just pack your bags and jump into the car and drive into the sunset. Holidays had to be planned and arrangements made for some colleague to take your services and the Parish office needed to be manned to register requests for baptisms or take bookings for weddings. Every priest was advised, however, to take a retreat once a year and a day off every week. Even so, that was not always possible; inevitably there was always something that cropped up which seemed to demand my attention. When I was at Cannock, I had a caravan pitched near Alton Towers in Staffordshire where I used to escape to for a couple of nights just to get away from the parish.

When I was in Dymchurch I took a few days off not so much for a holiday but to get away from the pressures of the job, which occasionally got me down especially when I was depressed and alone in the house. On one occasion I went up to Edinburgh with my friend, James, to see his twin brother, John. I remember that I could not stay with them at John's bungalow, so I had to put up at a hotel somewhere nearby. Whilst there I met the Right Reverend Richard Holloway when he was the Primus of the Scottish Episcopal Church walking down Princes Street and I stopped him and asked if I could

203

come and talk to him. I had already been to the Sung Eucharist at St. Mary's Episcopal Cathedral the day before, so I had some idea of where he lived. We met by arrangement the next day and I told him that I was a closeted priest in the Church of England and suffered from bouts of depression. Recently I had had a bad time with a member of my congregation who threatened to expose me although he had no evidence. His grievance against me was because he had not been recommended by the Parish Council to go forward for training for the Local Ordained Ministry. Richard listened and shared my anguish and pain over the Churches' cruel stance on the homosexual issue and its monstrous hypocrisy. I thanked for his time and the empathy he had shown me. His final words to me which I shall never forget, 'Don't let the buggers get you down.'

* * *

Brett was a teenager who worshipped at All Saints, Burmarsh. He was a delightful young man who was very good at bringing the children from the village into the church. Towards the end of my time on Romney Marsh, I heard that he had left home and gone to London. I always wondered why, but of course, no one said anything. Around about 2005 when I was living at Charterhouse Almshouse in London, I happened to meet him again. Now in his late twenties, he was a nurse at St Bartholomew's Hospital. He and his boyfriend used to come to see me quite often; and then one day I learned that he had died quite suddenly of AIDS. I was absolutely shocked at the waste of such a lovely person's life. His boyfriend was devastated and I spent a lot of time trying to comfort him, but he seemed hell-bent on following Brett to the grave. Sadly, he too died shortly afterwards. He booked a room in a hotel for a night and next morning he was found dead. He had hanged himself. I attended both their funerals and read the lessons. It still troubles me, and I wonder if I had been open about my sexuality whether I could have helped Brett's parents to accept him as he was. But back then, people kept their thoughts and difficulties over homosexuality to themselves in a clandestine world and consequently were out of reach of help.

* * *

It is a common perception that people who go to church are holy and therefore good. The Saints of the Church are commemorated for their faithfulness to Christ not for their good deeds, although many of them also led exemplary lives. The Christian calling is about what we might become and not what we are now; in the meantime, we must contend with all the quirks and foibles of our human nature. I'm reminded of a clip from the film *Brokeback Mountain* when Ennis says to Jack Twist, 'if you can't fix it, you gotta stand it'. Just after I had been inducted Rector of SS. Peter and Paul in Dymchurch, a retired priest on the staff died. His widow, Dorothy, assumed that she had the same authority in church affairs that her husband had. I received several letters from her which criticised aspects of my behaviour as a priest. For instance, one day I found an old chest containing some vestments in a state of such disintegration that I threw them out. 'How dare you interfere with such sacred garments,' raged Dorothy in one of her letters. 'Did you not know that I am the wardrobe mistress?'

The church did not have running water and so water for the communion vessels had to be obtained from a tap in the churchyard used by people who put flowers on their loved ones' graves and the flower ladies who decorated the church. The sacristan was a very elderly lady who was no longer able to perform her duties: she was not washing the vessels properly and did not renew the water when setting up the altar for communion. Having fallen ill from drinking the dirty water, I gently relieved the sacristan of her duties. My, what a vituperative letter I got from Dorothy! Later, I learned from members of my congregation that her late husband, when not about his priestly duties, used to spend his spare time either sitting on the seafront or listening to the cricket in a parishioner's house because he could not stand his wife's bossy and officious manner.

* * *

One of the responsibilities that falls to a priest which has nothing to do with his religious duties is that of looking after the church buildings and fabric, as well as dealing with repairs and alterations. This also involves raising the money to execute the work and obtaining 'a faculty' – formal permission to make any repairs or alterations. In some parishes this can take considerable time and effort and become a distraction from the real issues, particularly where the fabric of medieval churches is concerned. I was engaged in two projects on Romney Marsh: one proved to be a constant thorn in the flesh and was not resolved during my time as a priest there; the other involved replacing the lighting at the church of SS. Peter and Paul in Dymchurch, which had not been touched since the 1930s. To raise the money, I volunteered to follow my churchwarden in my camper van while he cycled from Land's End to John O'Groats and back. My campervan became his mobile hotel, providing bed and board after his daily exertions. We raised sufficient money to install modern lighting in the church which transformed the ambience of the interior.

SS. Peter and Paul at Newchurch also had lighting problems: the wiring was faulty, and the fuses kept on blowing. I was informed that it was very dangerous and liable to cause a fire. Despite the urgency of the problem, the Diocese refused to grant a faculty until we had brought in specialists to examine the walls for hidden wall paintings. Such a procedure was very costly and there was no way at that time to raise more money to cover this additional expense. I was so worried about the potential fire risk that I instructed the contractor, who had given us a good quotation, to start the work. The Diocesan authorities came down on me like a ton of bricks, and I had to ask the contractor to cease the work pronto. This seemed crazy to me – the idea that preserving our heritage was more important than the safety of the building and the well-being of the congregation. Naturally, I ended up in the doghouse with both the contractor and the Diocese!

* * *

Before retiring as Rector of Dymchurch at the age of sixty-five I had to deal with a case of stalking. A priest who was brought up in Dymchurch and who used to return quite often to see his widowed mother continued to come back even after his mother had died. He was obsessed with a member of my congregation who had recently married. His attention caused this unfortunate woman a great deal of distress. He used to ring her from a telephone booth in view of her house, then wait for her to come out. He attended our services at the church so that he could see her and even asked if he could preach!

The congregation was unaware of what this priest was up to, especially my disaffected lay reader who accused me of being mean when I would not allow him to preach. The tragedy was that he had a lovely wife and a family in the West Country where he was still the parish priest. I confronted him about his behaviour and wrote to his Bishop who replied that as the priest was nearing retirement, he would not take any action. It struck me how odd it was that people tolerated heterosexual misdemeanours and yet got hot under the collar at the faintest whiff of homosexuality! I'm glad to say, however, that he never came again to terrify my parishioner, for which she was eternally grateful.

Before taking leave of Dymchurch I can't resist relating one more story. This time, about the renowned film director, artist and author Derek Jarman. As well as being very open about his homosexuality and his struggle with AIDS, he fought long and hard for gay rights. I first became aware of him in the '70s when I saw Ken Russell's film *The Devils*, for which Jarman designed the sets. Having read his first book on gardening, a passion that began as a young man, I went on to watch his films including *Sebastiáne*, in which the dialogue was delivered entirely in Latin, and *Caravaggio*, about the Italian Baroque painter. In 1986 after being diagnosed HIV positive, he moved to Prospect Cottage near Dungeness power station, just down the coast from Dymchurch. I used to take friends to look at the garden he had created out of flotsam and jetsam and salt-loving beach plants. At first, I was outraged and shocked at Jarman's frankness and openness about his homosexuality, but after getting to know more about his life I changed my mind and secretly admired him for his courage and honesty.

He died in 1994, two years after I had left Dymchurch. Although he was an atheist, Derek wished to be buried in St Clement's Church, Old Romney, where I had conducted services and preached many times. It is a delightful twelfth-century church with foundations dating back to the eighth century. It was here, rather than in Dymchurch, that the *Doctor Syn* film was made in 1962; a Walt Disney production which involved painting the box pews rose pink – they are still there. I understand that the Parochial Church Council viewed several of Jarman's films before giving permission for his burial. His grave is marked by a huge slate headstone on which is incised his signature.

* * *

Looking back on my time in the priesthood, I am constantly struck by what a privilege it was to share in the joys and sorrows of all the people who let me play a part in some of the most important, often life-changing, events in their lives: when they were married, when their children were born and brought for baptism, when they were sick and I visited them in hospital, when they were dying; and then officiating at their funerals and when their grieving relatives needed help and support. Of course, there was always the routine of daily prayers, arranging weekly services and preparing sermons; but for me, the greatest joy of being a priest was sharing people's problems and being given an opportunity to help them through their difficulties – the chance to bring something of the love of God to their notice; a love which enabled them to transcend their pain and move on in their lives.

Although less vehement than hitherto, the Church continues to show hostility towards homosexuals. Despite this and after so many years of hesitation (because of my homosexuality and depression), I am so glad that at long last I found the confidence and courage to become a priest. I wish that I had responded earlier to that inner voice which began to whisper in my ear when I was a teenager, but perhaps I was not ready. In view of my own difficulties and hang-ups, I remain in awe at how I have been sustained by the people to whom I was sent to minister and by the God whom I tried to serve. There is no doubt that my troubled life gave me some insight into other people's problems and enabled me to be of help to them. I did not always live up to their expectations and I wish that I had prayed more, listened more, visited more. When I left accountancy to become a priest, most people thought I had lost my senses, but the reverse was true: I gained far more than I gave up and would not have had it any other way.

Chapter 19

ISLAND IN THE SUN

In April 1992 I reached the age of sixty-five and soon after I retired from my living at Dymchurch. I still had lots of energy and did not feel ready to give up working life just yet. I had always wanted to live abroad, and I was aware that the Church of England had chaplains in most European cities as well as in the Middle East and the Far East. I saw in *The Church Times* that the Diocese in Europe required a chaplain for Menorca, one of the Balearic Islands. 'I'm not going there, it's too hot,' insisted my mother. I was in the dog house again. And she was up to her old tricks of trying to control me.

When she came to live with me in Dymchurch it was always understood that my brother and I would share the responsibility of caring for her after Aunty Win had virtually thrown her out. I told my brother of my plans to move to Menorca and he agreed that if I was offered the position mother could return and live with him and Doreen again. I went to see the Bishop responsible for European appointments at his headquarters in Kensington High Street, and after further interviews and the usual reference checks I was offered the position. After much thought, I accepted. A few weeks later my brother telephoned to tell me that he had changed his mind, muttering something about Doreen not being happy about mother going back to live with them. I was immediately thrown into a moral maze: my mother or Menorca?

After much soul-searching, I did something which I am still very troubled about. I put my ageing mother into a care home and went off to Menorca. Within a month of my departure, I had to return to the UK as mother had had a fall. Before returning to Menorca I took her out to tea one day in nearby New Romney and to have her glasses repaired as they had been damaged when she fell. During a conversation she suddenly said to me in a rather matter of fact way, 'I've had it yaw know, I'm worn out.' Within six weeks she had injured herself again more seriously this time, falling out of bed and fracturing her pelvis. Before I could get a flight back again, pneumonia had set in and she died in a small country hospital. It was uncanny; she seemed to know that her end was near. Hardly a day passes when I don't think of her, of something she used to do or say, some quotation from Shakespeare. She seems to be forever with me. I hope and pray that she is now at peace, free at last from all her anxieties and insecurities.

* * *

In July 1992 I flew to Menorca and took up residence in a church-rented apartment in the town of Es Castell, near to the Church of Santa Margareta. So began my life as the Chaplain to the English-speaking people who lived there. Although it was supposed to be a part-time job it was quite challenging, and I was as busy as I had been in the UK.

I was the first to establish a permanent Anglican chaplaincy on the island. Hitherto, people had received monthly visits from the chaplain in Majorca. The locals had rented a chapel building from the Roman Catholic parish church in Es Castell, about five kilometres from Mahon, the capital. The chapel, called Santa Margarita, had previously been used by an order of nuns who had run a school. During my time there I was invited to preach and share worship with the congregation at the parish church, and even shared the blessing with the Roman Catholic Bishop of Menorca.

* * *

I arrived to take up the chaplaincy in July, the hottest month of the year. The flat where I lived for the first few weeks was in the centre of Es Castell. The Spanish used to eat their *cena* ('evening meal') outside in their gardens in the cool of the evening, then stay up late into the night. I found it impossible to sleep while these gatherings were in progress, so I asked about renting somewhere else.

One of the visitors, a widowed lady, who came to the island every year for several weeks during the summer months owned a holiday villa in the countryside just outside Es Castell. In the grounds, there was a *casa pequeno* (small cottage) which was unoccupied all the year round. When she learned that the church was looking for a quieter place for the Chaplain to live, she kindly offered it to the church rent free. However, when the matter was discussed by the Church Wardens, they had reservations about the arrangements as the lady in question was, in their view, a troublemaker. It seemed that she was very critical of their management – especially the finances. Furthermore, the cottage needed renovating, especially requiring the installation of a stove. Despite these reservations, improvements were made, and I took up residence. I was very happy there and made the place as comfortable as I could and enjoyed the quietness of the countryside. Sadly, my peace was constantly spoilt by the lady owner who, when in residence, continued to complain to me about the church and I was unable to assure her that her criticism was unfounded. Nevertheless, she persisted, so I decided to vacate the cottage as I was not prepared to put up with this kind of behaviour any longer. The church ultimately bought a suitable flat near Es Castell where I enjoyed living for the rest of my time on the island. On reflection I think I was unwise to take up the offer of the cottage; I ought to have taken seriously the wardens' reservations, instead I made an embarrassing situation worse.

* * *

My congregation was a friendly crowd and made me very welcome. Most of them had come to retire in the sun, but there were also some who lived and worked on the island. During the summer the church was filled to overflowing on Sundays due to the influx of holiday-makers. I used to go to the hotels where the English visitors were staying to welcome them to the island and invite them to the Sunday service at Santa Margarita, no matter what their Christian allegiances were.

Every year a Synod was held in Madrid to which all the chaplains came from the newly formed Diocese in Europe; hitherto it had been called the Diocese of Fulham and Gibraltar which to Spanish ears was not very welcoming! While in Madrid we were hosted by an order of nuns who looked after us very well. I happened to be sick on one occasion and they were very kind to me.

I found the Spanish people charming and very friendly, and many of them came to worship at Santa Margarita. I attended Spanish lessons as soon as I arrived in Menorca, and it was not long before I took a service of baptism in Spanish. But for me the strangest experience was conducting funerals: instead of burial in the ground, the body was interred in a niche carved into the rock, reminiscent of Christ's burial in the tomb of Joseph of Arimathea.

Every week I used to write a religious article which was published in the English newspaper. I remember that one Sunday we held a special family service and I tailored my sermon for the younger members of the congregation using that delightful book *The Velveteen Rabbit* or *How Toys Became Real* by Margery Williams Bianco. Somehow the local Spanish press got wind of it and asked if they could translate my sermon for publication in Spanish.

* * *

My 'honeymoon' – as the first year in a new position is sometimes called – was marked by another of those experiences which I seemed destined to have. One of the regular worshippers was Mia, a very pleasant, middle-aged woman who lived in a large house in the countryside just outside Es Castell. Mia had been a companion to a rich lady who had died, and she was now waiting for the estate of the deceased to be wound up and the house sold.

I believe provision had been made for her to retire in some comfort. Until the house was sold, however, it was offered to the church for functions and I was also invited to stay there. How could I refuse, especially as the house had a private swimming pool? I vividly remember the night a pig which had strayed from the neighbouring field fell into the pool – it took several of us to rescue the poor thing!

Every year my lifelong friend James came to visit me in Menorca and on one occasion we were invited by Mia to stay with her for a few days at her time-share flat in Marbella. We spent a pleasant few days together before James and I went off to see the Alhambra Palace at Granada, followed by a trip to the rock of Gibraltar.

When I returned to Es Castell, I noticed that Mia was absent from the congregation for two or three Sundays running. I had a strange feeling that something was wrong but as I did not know what it was, I was in a quandary about what to do. Eventually I saw Mia at a function, but when I enquired after her, I was received very frostily indeed. Yes, it had happened again, she had fallen for me even though neither of us had ever given any indication of our feelings which as far I was concerned were that of a Christian friend and her pastor. I was never alone with Mia in Marbella because James was with me the whole time. I felt very sorry that this had happened again because she was an extremely pleasant person whom I liked very much.

The incident served as a warning regarding my own vulnerability: if I did not keep my own feelings in check something like this could happen to me, but with a man.

216

In fact, it nearly did. A member of the congregation, Clive, who had left Yorkshire and had come to Menorca with his family and had established a business here was interested in becoming a lay reader. I encouraged him in this matter and provided him with a course of reading and the appropriate books. We met quite regularly to discuss his progress and I found him very attractive – particularly as he had obviously thought a lot about his Christian calling. Of course, nothing happened; in any case, he was madly in love with his wife.

* * *

I enjoyed life on the island of Menorca, with its beautiful bays and countryside and Mediterranean climate. I liked the place because everything was on a smaller, more intimate scale compared to its larger relation, Majorca. Being a single man and a priest, my congregation became my family, especially as most of my 'real' family had died and I had fewer connections back home. I also liked the Menorcan people, who I found kind and very hospitable. I would have stayed much longer, but unfortunately the Irritable Bowel Syndrome (IBS) from which I had suffered for some years became more aggressive and after nineteen months I had to return to the UK for investigation and treatment.

I had one rather amusing incident before leaving the island, but again it had a rather sad side which revealed the sexual hang-ups some Christians still harbour. A young lady in my congregation, whom I had recently prepared for confirmation, kindly invited me to accompany her to the theatre in Es Castell. I suspected that she was a lesbian, and likewise I'm sure she suspected

I was a homosexual, but despite the tyranny of silence we still felt an unspoken connection. We arrived at the theatre to discover that the performance was a floor show featuring the most accomplished drag artists I had ever seen: young men dressed in superb costumes miming arias from Spanish Zarzuelas (the Spanish version of Italian Grand Opera). One of my churchwardens was shocked when he learned where I had been, alerting me to the fact that he and several other members of my congregation were very conservative in their views on homosexuality and other so-called variations.

Little did my churchwarden know that men who impersonate women are not necessarily homosexual and are not making a cultural statement about their sexuality but expressing their artistic sensibilities – one has only to think of Barry Humphries, creator of his famous alter ego Dame Edna Everage; he has been married four times and has four children.

* * *

Postscript: Since leaving Menorca in 1994 I have exchanged Christmas greetings and news with three couples who were members of my congregation at Santa Margaretta. Last year I had a visit from the present chaplain's church worker who informed me that they were planning to celebrate the twenty fifth anniversary of the full-time chaplaincy on the 3rd December 2017. In 1992 I went to Menorca to establish the Chaplaincy there and was the first full-time chaplain. So, I was invited to Menorca to share in these celebrations but during the previous few months I had experienced

problems with walking which prevented me from travelling, so sadly I had to decline the invitation.

Chapter 20

DYMCHURCH AGAIN

My mother often used to quote to me from Shake-speare's *As You Like It*:

All the world's a stage,
And all the men and women merely players;
They have their exits and their entrances,
And one man in his time plays many parts

Little did she realise how many parts I would play in my life: a jilted lover, a fool, a deceiver, a coward, a straight man, an accountant, a friar, a priest, a chaplain and finally a gay man and a Brother at Charterhouse. The burden of a double life was sometimes very hard to bear. Perhaps it would have been better to have been honest about sexuality and 'come out' to everyone right from the start. But in reality, it was not safe to do so until the 1990s and even then, the Church of England was still at war with itself and cannot reach a common mind about gay people.

* * *

In 1994 I left Menorca and returned to the UK, and took possession of the semi-detached house in Dymchurch I had bought just prior to leaving for Spain. The house was in Charles Cobb Close, named after one of my clerical predecessors who in 1867 swam out to rescue the only survivor of the *Courier de Dieppe*, a French ship which was floundering in a gale just off the coast of Dymchurch. He was awarded the Albert Medal for Lifesaving. As my public life as a priest was coming to an end, I made the momentous decision to gradually relax pretending to be a straight man. There is an unwritten rule in the Church of England that when a priest retires from his living, he should leave the parish to give the new incumbent a free hand. Since I had been absent from Dymchurch for two years I felt that I had given the new incumbent sufficient time and space not to offend against the rule. Although I attended the church where I had been Rector, I kept a very low profile, except when I was asked to take a funeral or the odd service when the priest was away.

Settling back in Dymchurch was quite difficult. I was still a single man and I did not have a friend to live with or a congregation to look after. I did not feel it was right to reconnect with people whom I had known when I was Rector as they were now someone else's responsibility. Sadly, my mother had died not long after I had left for Menorca, so I was alone and very lonely. For a while I was involved in bringing the house up to scratch as the tenant I had let the house to – a French engineer who worked on the Channel Tunnel – had left the place in a mess. Apparently, he had left the central heating on day and night at the highest temperature for several weeks and the boiler had packed up. Furthermore, he had neglected to pay the gas bill and consequently the supply was cut off. The Gas Board was still chasing him for payment of bills and I believe he was eventually taken to court. The garden was a wilderness, so I set about laying a lawn, making flower beds and growing tomatoes and melons as it was quite a suntrap.

As a retired priest, I was often invited by the wardens of other churches in the area to take services when there was an 'interregnum' (the time before a vacancy is filled). I must have preached and celebrated in most of the seventeen medieval churches on Romney Marsh.

One of the churches I often visited was All Saints, Lydd, a neighbouring village well known for its small airport from where you could fly to Le Touquet in fifteen minutes. All Saints boasted of having the longest nave in the county and its tall tower could be seen for miles around.

It was there I met Cecil, a retired accountant who lived in a beautiful cottage in High Street. A prominent couple in the congregation at All Saints, who were very vocal with their homophobic views, upset Cecil, so he left All Saints and went to the local Roman Catholic church at the other end of the village. A kind and generous man, Cecil invited a group of gay men known as the Ashford Gay Group to meet at his home where they were entertained with Cecil's superb cooking and hospitality. He invited me to join the group and I enjoyed their company very much. The members came from all walks of life – nurses, teachers, accountants, shop assistants; many were churchgoers; some held office in their churches and some were retired. Most of them had come to terms with their homosexuality. They had partners and lived together and seemed to have shrugged off the homophobia which was still rampant in places.

They were, to me, a breath of fresh air and I valued their friendship. The group met once each month, some of the wealthier members also hosted birthday parties and other special occasions at their homes.

* * *

My working life as a priest was a busy one and my life-style simple – especially when I was a Franciscan, which meant that I had little time or opportunity to provide properly for my retirement and old age. With this in mind, I returned to my old profession and offered my services to the local village accountant. As a result, I was able to enhance my modest finances and feel a little more secure.

My old friend James came to stay at Dymchurch quite regularly. One of our mutual friends, Richard, whom I had known since he came with his mother to see me about her tax affairs when I was an accountant in central London in the '70s, needed advice about his tax affairs so he became a regular visitor at Dymchurch too. He had been badly advised by his accountant, so it took a long time to regularise his affairs, but his visits enabled me to get to know him better and to deepen our friendship. Ken, a friend of Richard's, also wanted some tax advice so he joined the stream of visitors. As he lived locally, I introduced him to the Ashford Gay Group and we are still in touch to this day.

You will recall how Aunty Win, my mother's youngest sister, kicked my mother out of her house after persuading her to give up her own home; and how, later, she fell out with my brother Norman and his wife Doreen.

Despite her appalling behaviour, she still appealed to me to sort out her tax affairs, which her husband Chris had left in a terrible mess. I was faced with a moral dilemma. She had behaved badly towards members of my family, but she had never been objectionable to me. I could not forget what havoc she caused my mother in particular, but I agreed to help her nevertheless. Sorting out her financial affairs meant that I often had to drive up to the Black Country, where I always stayed with my brother and his wife – enjoying their hospitality but feeling like the enemy within.

It was obvious to me that Uncle Chris, the Master Butcher, had been up to his eyes in the Black Market during the fourteen years that meat was rationed (from January 1940 to July 1954). One of the first things Aunty Win confessed to me was that just before Uncle Chris died the pair of them had dug up £5,000 which they had buried under the floor of a downstairs toilet. They even had to buy a pickaxe because they'd covered the hole with concrete! Immediately after the exhumation, they lit a fire in their backyard and burnt the entire stash. You might well ask why? The answer is because this was 1971 and the UK had just introduced decimalisation, so they were afraid their bank would ask too many questions when they took the notes in for conversion. It was obvious that Aunty Win was not anxious to account to the tax man for her acquiescence in her husband's tax evasion but simply to clear her own conscience by her confessions to me – a priest! In any case, it was too late for the authorities to take any action as her husband had died and his business had closed long ago out of reach of statutory time limitations.

The next bombshell was the discovery that during the rationing period when Uncle Chris was in business, cash from the shop till had found its way into the hands of all the high-street building societies (this, of course, was before the building societies abandoned their mutual status and became limited liability companies). I remember the day when James and I went to their branches and presented the passbooks. The accounts had not been updated for interest for years and the tally was considerable, bearing in mind that probably neither the deposits or the accumulated interest had ever appeared on any income tax returns! Income Tax would, however, have been deducted from the interest at the source. On reflection, I can't help feeling that I spent too much of my time back in Dymchurch giving friends free tax advice, but perhaps this was a kind of substitute for my pastoral work as a priest!

* * *

I am jumping ahead of the next chapter in which I decide to retire properly and leave Dymchurch and move to London and join the band of Brothers at Charterhouse, an ancient almshouse. I was asked by the Rev. Roger Ellis, the then incumbent of SS. Peter and Paul to preach at the Parish Eucharist on the Sunday before I left. The year 2003 was when we entered that controversial war by invading Iraq and which led to the deposing of Saddam Hussein. On the religious front, there was the controversy which arose from the appointment of Canon Jeffery John, a gifted and well-loved cleric who

226

had pro-gay views, as the suffragan Bishop of Reading. Threats from the Evangelicals to withhold finance and from some of the overseas Bishops to break away forced Archbishop Rowan Williams to persuade Jeffrey John to withdraw his acceptance. I was also aware that the homophobic reader who caused me such grief and his family were still members of the congregation. Nevertheless, I was moved to say something about the destructive nature of holding extreme views. Problems in modern life are never simply black and white but are multi-faceted. Such extreme positions always lead to conflict, pain and destruction. I'm not much of a fan of pop music, but sometimes I have been grabbed by one or two of them when they speak to the heart. So, when I was writing my last sermon Bob Dylan's most famous song, 'Blowin' in the Wind', kept coming into my head. I understand that it came out in 1962 as a protest against the Vietnam War and has continued through its evocative tune and the metaphorical use of its lyrics to raise moral questions ever since. Here is the third line which asks the question, 'How many roads must a man walk down before you call him a man?' Originally aimed at the prejudices against hippies and drop outs, but I brought it up to date by adding homosexuals! Then follows the chorus line; Bob Dylan with his Jewish and Christian roots tell us that 'the answer, my friend, is blowin' in the wind'. A direct reference to the wind ('*Ruach*') of the Old Testament and the wind ('*Pneuma*') of the New Testament, to the spirit of God still blowing where it wills with no respect of persons. If only we would stop and listen to its message of love and peace. Who can tell what would happen when love is in the air!

During the sermon I played excerpts from the sound track of Bob Dylan singing his immortal song. To my amazement when I had finished, I was given a standing ovation!

Chapter 21

BAND OF BROTHERS

By the year 2000, I had been living on my own in Dymchurch for six years. Although I had made new friends since returning from Spain and renewed old friendships, I was still lonely, and I longed to settle down with a partner. I was deeply attached to James and Richard, but they did not share my need to live with someone on a permanent basis, they enjoyed their own space and were far too fixed in their own habits to change now. I also realised that at my time of life – having reached the age of seventy-three – the chances of finding a partner were pretty slim.

Throughout most of the twentieth century, it was not acceptable for male couples to set up house together – certainly not in a vicarage! – a situation created by the homophobia of the church and our society. Consequently, I have spent most of my life living alone, making my way in the world without the support of another. I remember one of the Brothers at Charterhouse telling me that when he and his lover tried living together late in life it ended their relationship. In a recent book, *Insomniac City*, Bill Hayes tells the story of his tender love affair with Oliver Sacks, the renowned neurologist. Oliver was seventy-five when he met Bill and had not had any involvement with another man since he was thirty. Both valued their space so highly that they decided not to share a flat together.

I remember that I was so depressed about my existential sense of loneliness that I went on a retreat in the hope that I might find someone who understood my situation. I can't remember whether it was on this occasion or some other event when I met Richard Kirker, former General Secretary of OneBodyOneFaith (formerly the Lesbian and Gay Christian Movement). It was he who suggested that I apply to become a Brother at the Charterhouse, a four-hundred-year-old almshouse near the Barbican, just outside the City of London.

One of my congregation in Menorca, a former Admiral, had retired to Morden College, Blackheath, after suffering a stroke. I did think of applying there, but I did not fancy being so far out of London, so I applied to the Charterhouse instead. Happily, I satisfied the criteria for application: I was over sixty, male, single, in reasonably good health, with modest income and capital, happy to share in communal life and able to pay the current modest monthly accommodation charge.

After several visits and interviews with Dr James Thomson, the Master of the almshouse responsible for the welfare of the Brothers and the management of the staff, and the Preacher, the Rev. Michael Stevens, I was accepted as a Brother.

On the 17th August 2003 I arrived at Charterhouse with my personal belongings, a few books, two pieces of furniture, and a bed. Such downsizing was necessary because the only accommodation available at the time was a tiny studio flat on the ground floor in the Admiral Ashmore Building, which had only recently been opened. Leaving most of my possessions behind was a wrench, but a year later I moved to a more commodious flat and have never been happier.

* * *

The extraordinary story of the Charterhouse began in 1348 when the land was bought to bury the victims of the Black Death as the local churchyards were already full. In 1371, Sir Walter de Manny established the London Charterhouse to house twenty-four Carthusian monks and a prior whose rules of life included silence and contemplation. In 1535 Henry VIII declared himself the Supreme Head of the Church, dissolved the monasteries and martyred those who opposed the Act of Parliament. In 1542, Lord North bought the site from the Commissioners and from the stones of the Carthusian chapel and the monks' cells built a Tudor mansion which became a home for wealthy noblemen and a refuge for royalty.

In 1611, Thomas Sutton bought the site and buildings and set up a foundation that now bears his name. This provided a home for up to eighty Brothers – 'either decrepit or old captaynes either at sea or at land, maimed or disabled soldiers, merchants fallen on hard times, those ruined by shipwreck or other calamity' – as well as the setting up of Charterhouse School for forty impoverished boys, known as 'Gown Boys'. When Sutton died a few months later, his will endowed the charity with a considerable sum of money – perhaps the largest ever recorded at the time.

James the First became the first Royal Governor of Thomas Sutton's foundation. Wellington, Gladstone and Cromwell have all been Governors, and the Charterhouse appears in the writings of Daniel Defoe, Charles Dickens and William Makepeace Thackeray. John Wesley, the founder of Methodism, was educated at the school between 1714 and 1720, which somehow makes me feel an added sense of connection given my strong Methodist background.

In 1872 the school moved to Godalming, but the Brothers remained at the Charterhouse in Clerkenwell. During the Blitz in May 1941, the buildings were gutted by fire from incendiary bombs and the Brothers were evacuated to Godalming. After WWII the Charterhouse was restored to its former glory and during the 1950s the Brothers returned to live in the Tudor house. The Charterhouse is now a registered charity. Her Majesty the Queen and members of the Royal Family are Royal Governors and the management is vested in fifteen trustees who are also called Governors.

In 2017, part of the buildings were converted into a public museum tracing the development of the Charterhouse over its six-hundred-year history and showcasing exhibits from its collection of paintings and artefacts. Tours are also available to see the beautiful gardens and the very spot where the offside rule in football originated – in the stunning cloister dating back to 1371 in which the boys of Charterhouse School first implemented the rule that made goal hangers extinct.

* * *

From my viewpoint, the location of the Charterhouse is without equal. We are next door to the Barbican Centre with its cinemas, concert halls and library. The West End is within easy reach by bus or tube. The Museum of London is on our doorstep and the British Museum and Art Galleries are close by. It is situated on the edge of the City of London and within easy reach of the large London hospitals, doctors' surgeries and chemists.

Again, in my view, the lifestyle which the Charterhouse affords to its residents could not be surpassed. There is little by way of rules except those demanded by courtesy and respect for others. Meals are served at prescribed times: breakfast buffet-style from 08.15 to 09.00; formal lunch with Grace at 13.00; tea at 15.40 (if you want to put on weight!) and supper buffet-style at 18.15. Absence from meals and the taking of holidays must be logged with the management, and guest accommodation can be booked according to availability. Brothers can invite guests to lunch by arrangement. There is now a scheme of support for Brothers who may be temporarily indisposed or who need help with shopping or accompanying to the hospital. There is also an infirmary offering full-time care for those Brothers who have become too frail to look after themselves, as well as plans to extend domiciliary care to those brothers living independently. A physiotherapist comes twice a week to work with Brothers who have restricted mobility, while an osteopath, a chiropodist and a barber are available by appointment at reduced fees.

The Charterhouse has an interesting and varied programme of social events; including a garden party in

July, the Brothers' Founder's Lunch in November, and a Founder's Day Service and Dinner in December. Eminent speakers are invited to lecture on topical subjects, while musicians and singers regularly give recitals which are also open to the public.

We have our own reading group, choosing and discussing a wide variety of books and sometimes inviting the authors to come and present their work. Our monthly poetry group is led by Brother Gordon, a former lieder singer and actor who keeps us entertained with his insatiable appetite for jokes and funny stories. Games of bridge and chess are part of the fabric of life for many of the Brothers, while a daily supply of newspapers and an ever-expanding library help to keep our minds open and occupied.

Our chaplain (traditionally called the Preacher) leads Morning and Evening Prayer every day in the Jacobean Chapel created out of the Carthusian Chapter House. It is here that we also celebrate Holy Communion on Sundays and Feast Days. When the Preacher is away, the Brothers who have retired from their livings dust off their robes and step up to the pulpit.

In 2018, the first woman was admitted to the almshouse. Currently, there are forty-four Brothers at the Charterhouse. Four of them are living in the infirmary, while the remainder of us live in self-contained flats with our own shower and toilet. Some also have cooking facilities and a small refrigerator, enabling Brothers to self-cater instead of eating in the Great Hall. I value this facility very much as it enables me to entertain Richard and James on their weekly visits.

The Brothers come from all walks of life and hold a wide range of views about life, politics and religion. At present there are priests, lawyers, teachers, actors, an organist, singers, a publisher, a ballet correspondent, a diplomat and businessmen. Such a mix of professions produces stimulating table talk, a fount of knowledge and experience which enriches and broadens one's own life and stimulates mutual interests – and, of course, a lot of banter. Such sharing has rekindled my love of poetry and reading, and my knowledge of history and theology have undergone a reformation. Best of all, I have found many friendships and much camaraderie.

As one would expect in any community, there is the odd person who can be difficult or irritating: one Brother who sat at my table used to wash his dentures in his teacup and stick his head in *The Times* throughout the whole of breakfast; another elderly gentleman used to invite Brothers to his flat for a drink and greet them in the nude – he also came to meals dressed only in sandals, hot pants and a sports shirt! Living in a community demands a sense of humour, tolerance and, above all, sensitivity.

* * *

With King's College London right on our doorstep and time on my hands, I thought of taking a degree in Theology, Psychology and Sociology. Instead, encouraged by our former Master James Thomson, I became involved in a seven-year-long visual arts project! The Charterhouse was a cornucopia of portraits of the great and the good; paintings, drawings, watercolours, lithoprints and photographs, as well as artefacts and memorabilia donated throughout its long history. One day, I suggested it would be helpful to have a catalogue of all these treasures. No sooner had I opened my mouth than I was climbing the steep learning curve that would eventually lead to the production of a handbook containing over six hundred digital images with biographical notes on the sitters and the artists, and historical notes to assist the storyline.

During my school days I had produced a *History of Oldbury,* where I was brought up, and I had also spent four years working as a compositor, so printing was in my blood – but, of course, that technology was now obsolete. Fortunately, my friend, Richard, who was skilled in computers and digital photography came to the rescue. We soon learnt that only the very large portraits lent themselves to photographic reproduction, so I purchased a large scanner and a coloured printer to reproduce the smaller pictures. I did the research, restoration and the editing, while Richard masterminded the layout, presentation and the comprehensive index. Finally, Richard prepared a PowerPoint presentation of the book which was shown to an invited audience to launch the book, an event during the celebrations to mark the Charterhouse Quatercentenary celebrations in 2011. A second edition followed in 2013 which included more information, plus the pictures and artefacts which had been donated since the original publication. *The Handbook and Guide to Charterhouse Art 2013* provides invaluable information for those wanting to know what the Charterhouse has to offer.

* * *

In the haven of the Charterhouse where being a homosexual was no longer an issue, I luxuriated in my new-found freedom to 'be me'. But outside those ancient walls, the past still hung on with bony fingers. While writing the Charterhouse handbook I still visited my Aunty Win, who by this time was housebound and looked after by carers. Until she died at the age of ninety-two, I returned to the Black Country three or four times a year to celebrate her birthday, to look after her financial affairs, and to give her carers a break.

One of the things that shocked me when I was standing in for the carers was how unhygienic Aunty Win was in her personal habits, although I should have expected nothing less given the general perversity of her behaviour. I was always aware that she had bad breath caused by a gum disease known as gingivitis, but she refused even when she was mobile to go to the dentist for treatment. I also discovered that she wore her underclothes day and night and would not let the carers wash them more frequently than once a week even though they were badly soiled. Nor would she ever allow her carers to give her a bed bath. Her morning ablutions consisted solely of wiping her face with a flannel and slapping on a bit of Ulay, and she remained a stranger to the modern bathroom and shower that she'd insisted on installing. Even now I can hear her proclaiming, 'Them baths tek all the oil out of yaw skin.' She was equally unimpressed with the talcum powder her friends gave her for Christmas, insisting that it 'stopped up yer pores' and throwing the gifts straight in the dust-bin. Ironically, if anyone ever mentioned sex in any context, she would immediately declaim it as 'filth' and kill the conversation stone dead (judging by this, I suspect her husband did not have much fun in the bedroom). The final shock about her hygiene came not from my aunt but from her wardrobe, which was still in the room where I slept on my visits. My aunt had moved out of her bedroom when she got too lame to climb the stairs. I remember the first time I opened the wardrobe door I was knocked back by the stink! It was jammed full of dresses, including some very expensive evening gowns which probably had never been washed or cleaned.

Believe it or not there seems to be a royal precedent for Aunty Win's general behaviour and attitude to hygiene, as I discovered when I came across this description of Caroline of Brunswick, who married (disastrously) George IV. As Lord Malmesbury, who escorted Princess Caroline from Brunswick to England to meet Prince George, recorded in his diary:

'She lacked judgement, decorum and tact, spoke her mind too readily, acted indiscreetly and often neglected to wash or change her dirty clothes.' Lord Malmesbury is also reputed to have said that when George IV first saw his bride-to-be, he was so taken aback that he asked for a stiff drink. Uncanny.

Even in her very old age Aunty Win was still impulsive, vindictive and quarrelsome, and still having her periodic spats with her so-called friends. Whenever they upset her too much, she would cut them out of her will and find someone else on whom to bestow her largesse. Even when she was critically ill in hospital and I had to return to London, she asked the nurse to ring me to arrange for a solicitor to go to the hospital and remove some unfortunate soul from her will, to the benefit of another. She left a legacy to my friend James, but when I was winding up her estate, I discovered that she had given half of it to someone else!

Aunty Win's carers were a foreign couple who made themselves indispensable to her; to my knowledge, she paid off their mortgage, gave them a car and left them the house in her will. During my administration of her estate, the carers engaged a solicitor who queried as to why I was taking so long in conveying the house to them! She left me a very reduced legacy and I immediately made a Deed of Variation in favour of my brother for a share of it, as she had cut him and my mother out of her will in the great fallout. I realise now that my aunt used her wealth to exert power over people, offering financial carrots which she could dangle or withdraw on a whim.

In the early days I used to travel from Dymchurch to the Black Country in my car, which by this time was on its last legs, or wheels to be precise. I had no interest in cars other than their ability to get me from one place to another. For years I drove a cheap, yellow Citroën car; the radiator was faulty, and my parishioners used to call it a 'travelling refrigerator'. Aunty Win, however, insisted that I traded my car in at the local dealers for a swanky Rover saloon, for which she paid the difference. On the return journey to Dymchurch, I had a near-death experience I shall never forget.

The famous Romney Hythe and Dymchurch Railway runs parallel to the coast from Dungeness to Hythe. To get to the coast I had to cross the railway line at a point where the hedgerows, in the full bloom of summertime, had obscured the warning lights. Weary after the long journey and lulled by the smooth running of my new car, I crossed the railway line just before the train sped through the cutting. A second later and the train would have smashed into the car, killing me outright and causing God knows what damage to the train and unspeakable horrors for its passengers. As the train rocketed past, my heart pumped so hard from fear I thought it would burst from my chest.

This was the second time I have lived to tell the tale after a near-fatal car accident. Many years previously, when I was in practice as an accountant, I used to drive up the A1 to Newark-on-Trent and then cut across country to Mansfield to see clients. The Great North Road links London with Edinburgh and many sections incorporate old Roman roads, so much of it is straight and driving can be very boring. Approaching the village of Long Bennington, five miles south of Newark where there is a huge bend, I was suddenly aware that the Mini I was driving was veering off the road into the fields ahead. I jammed on the brakes so violently that the car screeched into a U-turn worthy of a Hollywood stunt just at the point where there was a break in the central reservation, and I found myself hurtling down the A1 in the opposite direction towards London. Fortunately, there was no traffic travelling south. I have never ceased to wonder who was looking after me.

Clearly angling for another hand-out, Aunty Win's carers told me that they could not visit her so often without proper transport. So, I made my last ever journey to the

Black Country by road, handed over the posh Rover Saloon which aunty Win had given me to the carers and gave up driving for good. Thereafter I went by train to Langley Green in the Black Country to see my aunt until her death in 2007. Aunty Win's death was a very sad affair. Mainly because it was, in part, of her own making. My discovery of her poor hygiene when I was standing in for her untrained carers was not a consequence of growing old but to a large extent had been her own lifestyle choice. Despite having a modern bathroom and shower she continued to wash at the kitchen sink, cat licking as my mother used to call it. When she lost her mobility and was confined to her chair and latterly to her bed, personal care was minimal. She repeatedly became infected resulting in breathing problems. Furthermore, had her carers, who were aware of my aunt's vindictive nature, made any attempt to insist on better hygienic habits they may well have got their marching orders!

She was admitted to hospital on several occasions where she then caught the MRSA super bug. Ultimately, she was transferred to a Geriatric Hospital, where the doctor said that they were unable to control her many infections. He suggested that I let nature take its course. She had many other physical problems which made life very difficult, but none were life-threatening. There was certainly nothing wrong with her mind, she was still as sharp as ever. On my last visit to see her, she was beginning to sink. Nevertheless, she held up her left hand and pointed to the ring on her finger. On closer examination, I noticed that both her wedding and engagement rings had been removed and in their place

241

was a very thin cheap gold-plated ring. I can only conclude that as she lost weight it became possible to remove her rings and substitute this cheap one. I knew that when she went into hospital it was impossible to take the rings off her finger without hurting her. It was obvious that someone had stolen her rings which were quite valuable and replaced them with a fake. I took this up with the management, but they would have none it, and refused to believe that there was a thief on the ward! She died two weeks later at the age of ninety-two. On her death certificate, it was stated that sepsis was the primary cause of death.

* * *

Aunty Win was the last of my aunts to die. Uncle Gilbert, who married my father's youngest sister, Tilly, was the last of my uncles to die, at the age of ninety-eight. When WWII broke out in September 1939, Uncle Gil and Aunty Tilly were on their honeymoon in the Black Forest in Germany and had to return to the UK in a hurry. Unfortunately, they were unable to have any children of their own, so they adopted a boy named Michael and a girl named Helen. A Mancunian with a degree in Engineering from Manchester University, Uncle Gil spent most of his adult life developing and servicing submersible pumps all over the world – whether supplying petrol stations, irrigating waterless wastes, draining mines shafts or installing oil rigs in the North Sea. My brother Norman's stamp collection was considerably increased by the foreign stamps from Uncle Gil's correspondence. When not working, Uncle Gil devoted his time to the Air Training Corp as a Wing Commander.

I have fond memories of Uncle Gil: as a boy he would take me on long walks across the local golf course, talking to me with warmth and understanding. He also liked classical music and had a huge collection of vinyl records. My parents used to take Norman and me to visit our aunt and uncle in their new house which they bought soon after they married. It was like heaven: carpeted floors, rooms lit by electric light, running hot and cold water. I remember distinctly that the house was always warm – all the downstairs rooms opened into the hallway which meant that when you opened the front door the heat did not escape. Best of all, they had a radiogram, and it was there that I first heard the glorious sounds of Italian opera singers and the magical music of Mozart and Beethoven. That radiogram was still there seventy years later when I visited his house in Horsham after his death.

Uncle Gil appointed me as the executor of his will because his son Michael, a communications wizard, had lived in the States for many years after being headhunted by American Airways; sadly, his daughter Helen was born deaf and was unable to undertake such a responsibility.

* * *

I suppose it is to be expected that when one reaches my sort of age, death becomes a constant fact of life. It has certainly seemed so while living at the Charterhouse. The most recent family death occurred about two years ago when my brother's wife, Doreen, died in her mid-eighties after suffering from Alzheimer's – a cruel death to be sure. Norman and Doreen were a devoted couple, but sadly they could not have any children of their own. Taught by our parents in early life not to show any emotion and to keep a stiff upper lip, my brother is finding it very difficult to come to terms with Doreen's death, especially having so few friends with whom to share his pain. When I was ill with pneumonia and pleurisy two years ago, Norman sadly acknowledged that he would be left alone if I was to die first.

My mother was similarly affected when my father died. She could not cry or sleep and became quite ill. It was the early '70s and James and I had just bought our house in Ealing, so mother came to stay with us for a while. We took her to see a consultant who sorted out a host of medical problems and tried to counsel her through her grief. I found it difficult to grieve for my father and I still have nightmares about my mother's death even after twenty-five years. Recently, Prince Harry revealed how he suppressed his grief for many years after the death of his mother, Princess Diana. Keeping things bottled up can have a devastating effect on one's mental health, but it seems that it still takes a figure as well-known as Prince Harry to highlight this fact and acknowledge that we are all just human beings in need of solace and comfort when we experience loss.

* * *

I was ninety years old on April 4th, 2017. My lifelong friends James and Richard wanted to mark the occasion by hosting a party at Charterhouse. Because I had an appointment at the hospital near to the 4th a lunch party was arranged for April 10th in the Queen Elizabeth Day Room, followed by a visit to the recently opened Charterhouse Museum. It was a splendid occasion, with forty guests gathering for drinks, with a buffet lunch and birthday cake prepared by Alan, our master chef. Along with my fellow Brothers and friends I have known for many years, my cousin, Michael and his wife, Margaret came from Denver, Colorado, and my brother Norman came down from the Black Country. I was moved and delighted to be surrounded by so many friends at my time of life.

Before bringing this chapter on life at the Charterhouse to an end, there are two events which took place in my ninetieth year which brought some closure to two issues which had greatly troubled me when I was a young man. The first concerned exorcism now included in a blanket term 'conversion therapy'; the second concerned the threat of prosecution if the authorities had discovered I'd had a love affair with another young man in the '40s.

I read in the *Church Times* that a motion was to be put forward at the Church of England Synod meeting in York in July 2017 condemning the practice of conversion therapy. In a letter to the lay representative for the Diocese of Oxford who was proposing the motion, I related my experience of many of these therapies which did not work and caused me considerable suffering and distress. My letter was read before the motion was put to the vote, which was carried by all three houses of the Synod. (see Appendix)

Earlier in 2017, I was invited by the BBC to take part in a documentary film based on Peter Wildeblood's book *Against the Law*, which tells the story of Wildeblood's love affair with another man for which he was prosecuted and sent to prison. I read the book in my mid-twenties, just before my breakdown, and was terrified by the knowledge that I too had had a love affair with another man and that according to the law I was a criminal too. Furthermore, it was at the same time when the Church was becoming more vocal on the issue, saying that I was also 'an abomination to God'; and finally, according to some new thinking by the medical profession, that homosexuality was a 'mental illness' rather than a terrible sin. The film was produced to mark the fiftieth anniversary of the passing of the Sexual Offences Act in 1967 which decriminalised homosexual acts between two consenting men. It was shown on BBC2 on 26th July 2017. I featured in the film and was able to share what it felt like to be a potential criminal. It is of some comfort to know that also in January 2017 some 49,000 men were posthumously pardoned under the terms of the Policing and Crime Act 2017'.

Chapter 22

COMING OUT

I have found telling parts of my story a very painful experience. Other parts have been a great pleasure. I have tried to be honest and have held nothing back to prevent any misunderstanding. I hope that I have not protested too much. Even though I am glad that I struggled to educate myself, I regret that I did not go to university, despite gaining the necessary qualifications to take an external degree. I was able to free myself from the factory labour trap in which most working-class people were snared and to earn more than my father did. This enabled me to live a fuller life, see something of the world and meet many interesting people.

I was born homosexual. I did not choose it. I have spent much of my life wishing that I had been born straight. I do not hold my parents responsible for who I am or that I grew up in a hostile, bigoted and ignorant world riddled with prejudices, poverty and class distinctions. I certainly do not believe that being a homosexual is evil or against the natural order of things, as many Fundamentalist Christians claim. Humans have a poor record of coping with differences and yet it is our very differences or uniqueness which is the mark of our Creator, who created us to love and to relate to one another. I am simply a human being who is attracted to men rather than women. I am very sad that the Church of England, which I have served in one capacity or another for the last sixty years, has been so slow to accept homosexuals.

This is baffling as the church has so many homosexuals in its ranks of ordained priests and consecrated bishops. It is even more baffling why so many homosexuals offer themselves for ordination knowing that they cannot marry their partner without putting themselves out of a job if the Bishop applies the existing rules; surely God must be somewhere in all this confusion and hypocrisy?

I believe that the Church has missed a great opportunity to show Christ-like compassion and understanding towards gay people and could have saved many from suffering and suicide. This is even more astonishing as the Christian Church has many fine theologians who have written about homosexuality in a positive way; some of their writings are mentioned in my bibliography. Recently I read online the obituary of the late Anthony Dyson, who was Professor of Social and Pastoral Theology at Manchester University. His career was characterised by the conviction that academic theology and the churches alike could expect no credibility in the modern world without seriously engaging with other insights into the human condition! I regret that I had to wait so long for the changes which began to take place later in my life, and my struggle in coming to terms with my homosexuality and the crippling depression which the trauma brought about had lasted so long.

When my brother and I were young, my mother often used to quote to us the proverb popularised by William Hickson:

If at first you don't succeed,
Try, try, try again.

I did try, try and try again to change, but nothing worked. My mother always said that I was an idealist and I suppose that's the reason why I persevered for so long in trying to find a cure for my homosexuality – despite it becoming clear that things were never going to change. It would have been better to accept who I was at a much earlier stage.

I regret very much that I was deprived of a normal sex life, something which caused me a lot of frustration. I longed to be able to love a woman and have children – I hope that I would have made a better job of them than my parents did of me. I have experienced love and had some intimate male relationships, but these could not flourish in such a cold climate. There was too much prejudice and guilt around. I would have liked to have had a loving relationship with another man and to live together, free from the homophobia spread by Church and State before the law was changed. I have never felt self-contained and happy in my own skin because I could not rid myself of nagging regrets and anxieties. I enjoyed being a priest and found it a fulfilling vocation, but the loneliness was sometimes hard to bear. As the Bible states in a line which has always echoed in my mind: 'It is not good for man to be alone' (Genesis 2:18).

* * *

In recounting these experiences of a repressed gay man, I realise that I have also been on a kind of journey, a search for meaning and clarification of life itself. Digging deeper into psychology, sociology, history and theology has certainly helped me to make sense of my life and the world in which I grew up. Above all, I now feel that I can finally answer the question which Alice asked herself when she was down the rabbit hole: 'Who am I?' From an early age, I recognised that I was not normal as the world understood normality. I was different, but I could not accept that difference and neither could many other people. The consequence of not being able to accept who I was and being rejected by others resulted in the construction of another me, another self – a false self. My first tactic, although subconscious, was to use the defence mechanism of repression: pushing the feelings of shame and anger which I could not face down into my unconscious. By living a double life, I consciously suppressed and denied my homosexuality – both to myself, to others and to God. I internalised my homosexuality so that it became a kind of wound disguised by the sticking plaster of acting the part of a straight man.

The difficult ascent towards accepting the truth about myself has been accomplished through a ruthless process of questioning and self-examination. This has gradually uncovered the deeply embedded falsehoods and untruths that hardened over the years into a second skin. Writing this autobiography has been an honest attempt to come clean and has released the locked-up anger and frustration I felt for years. It has enabled me to see the illusions for what they were, to recognise the folly of keeping up appearances and to admit to myself that I am simply one of God's creatures who happens to be a gay man. It has been like peeling away the layers of an onion, to discover the real me at the centre of my being. I have indeed experienced a catharsis, freedom from the need to suppress my homosexuality and to waste my energies in keeping up appearances. I no longer feel guilty or ashamed of my sexual orientation. At the age of ninety-one, I, Stanley Underhill, have given myself leave to be myself, to be content with who I really am. I suppose, with retrospect, I have at last been able to take the advice that Polonius offered to his son, Laertes, in Shakespeare's Hamlet to heart: 'This above all, to thine own self be true.'

* * *

'Pull yourself together, man.' For years, this was the order I heard. Well-meant, of course, but totally inappropriate when one is locked inside that dark cloud called 'depression' and there is no wind to blow it away. To a large degree that cloud which enshrouded me for so long and with such debilitating effects has largely evaporated.

It still bothers me that depression is such a pervasive condition and yet the medical profession has not cracked it, despite all the new drugs and treatments which are available. Thankfully, the stigma attached to 'seeing a shrink' or spending time in a psychiatric ward has declined in recent years. We have seen the proliferation of enlightened therapists and counsellors offering positive therapies for all kinds of mental disorders and addictions. On one level the proliferation of mental health problems is terrifying, but, at the same time, it is comforting to know that there are humane and knowledgeable people out there who are ready to listen to us. Unfortunately, however, there is still a lot of stigma attached to those who suffer from more serious mental conditions and those who attempt suicide. Much

251

more research is needed to identify the causes of depression and why people are driven to end their lives.

Undoubtedly, living at Charterhouse for the past fifteen years has contributed enormously to my rehabilitation. It has enabled me to 'come out', as they say, and to make so many friends. For this and so much more, I shall be eternally grateful.

Chapter 23

I WILL SURVIVE

'I Will Survive', released in 1978 and written by Freddie Perren and Dino Fekaris, is a pop song about the discovery of personal strength following a devastating break-up. It sold millions of copies worldwide and has remained a popular tune and gay anthem ever since. Backed by stirring horns and strings, the American vocalist Gloria Gaynor interprets the lyrics with great emotional power. The song has always struck a deep and lasting chord with me and has sustained me in writing this book.

I have spent the last years of my life at Charterhouse writing this autobiography and its underlying theme in a word has been that of 'survival'. I survived bullying at school and verbal bullying from my father. I survived an exorcism by my misguided and erstwhile Christian lover, followed by a mental breakdown for which I was given Electric Current Therapy. I survived a series of so-called 'cures' for my homosexuality, including testosterone injections and lithium – all of which failed to redirect my sexual inclinations.

I survived the stigma of having been in a mental institution and losing my job. I survived a Freudian shrink who pulled me apart and left me like Humpty Dumpty after his great fall.

I survived long and short bouts of depression which have punctuated most of my life and the medications which made me feel like a zombie.

I survived the possibility of being sent to prison by the State for loving a man and the bigotry of Fundamentalist Christians. I survived near-bankruptcy when I was an accountant and suffered the cruel treatment of colleagues who objected to my homosexuality. I survived the temptations to run away from my problems and to commit suicide. I risked 'outing' when pretending to be a straight man.

When I was ordained a priest in the Church of England, I suffered threats from members of the congregation even though I never disclosed my homosexuality. I have also survived several other natural disasters during my ninety-one years on this planet earth.

I have pondered long, hard and deep as to why I have survived, and have concluded that God does not so much deliver us from our problems but carries us through them. I suppose that I am a lucky chap. Every time I hear the Perren and Fekaris pop song *I will survive*, I am reminded of another lucky chap, Job, who after all his trials and tribulations cries out in a great act of faith, 'I know that my Vindicator lives' (Job 19.25) in whose face, I see love.

Although I have come to the end of my story and will soon hit the 'save' key on the computer for the last time, it is still not the end. I shall continue to explore the mystery of who I was, who I am, and who I might still become. I've always been fascinated by the poetry of T. S.

Eliot, who believed that suffering was needed for all of society before new life could begin. In the last of his *Four Quartets* he brings the question of time and human destiny to a conclusion. So, let me bring my story to a conclusion with the line from 'Little Gidding': 'And the end of all our exploring will be to arrive where we started.'

And finally, some words taken from the writings of Julian of Norwich – a fourteenth-century Christian Mystic and Theologian:

And all shall be well and
All manner of things shall be well.

THE END

Postscript

I never thought for one moment that I would leave Charterhouse. I was convinced that I would die there. Charterhouse accepted me when I was a very unhappy man. It provided me with the space to come to terms with my sexuality which had troubled me for most of my life. It also gave me the confidence and encouragement to write this autobiography, for which I shall always be grateful. The reassurance I received from the feedback of my publication opened up my world afresh. Living at Charterhouse provided opportunities to talk about my problems, make new friends and pursue new interests, all of which gave me the freedom to enjoy my life as never before.

However, all of this ended abruptly when the first lockdown, caused by the Covid crisis, was enforced. After weeks of being forced into virtual solitary confinement, I gradually realised that I would like to live independently again. My friend James, who was then 98, needed support and I thought that it be would be good to live nearer to him.

I recalled the late Canon Eric James quoting in a sermon, a line from T. S. Eliot's *East Coker: "Old men ought to be explorers"*. This had stuck in my mind ever since and so, on the 28th of August 2020, my life changed once again: I left Charterhouse and moved to the same block of retirement flats where James has lived for many years now.

258

Bibliography

All of the books listed below have affected me – often profoundly – and helped me to make sense of the world. Most are still in print or available second-hand. Where possible I have listed the most recent edition and included the year of original publication. Happy hunting!

AELRED, of Rievaulx. Spiritual Friendship. Cistercian Publications, 2010. (original manuscript 1164-67).

BAILEY, Derrick Sherwin. Homosexuality and the Western Christian Tradition. Longmans, Green, 1955.

BARR, Damian. Maggie and Me. Bloomsbury, 2013.

BATTEN, Rex. Rid England of This Plague. Paradise Press, 2005.

BEECHING, Vicky Undivided. William Collins, 2018.

BLOCH, Michael. The Life of James Lees-Milne. John Murray, 2009.

BOSWELL, John. Same-Sex Unions in Premodern Europe. Villard Books, New York 1994.

BRYANT Christopher. Depth Psychology and Religious Belief. Mirfield, 1977.

BRYANT, Christopher. The River Within. Darton, Longman & Todd, 1978.

COLES, Richard (Rev.). Fathomless Riches. Weidenfeld & Nicolson, 2014.

CONLEY, Garrard. Boy Erased. William Collins, 2016.

DOMINION, Jack (Dr.). Cycles of Affirmation. Darton, Longman & Todd, 1975.

DOMINION, Jack (Dr.). Depression. Fontana, 1976.

DOWD, Mark. Queer and Catholic, Darton, Longman and Todd, 2017.

DOWNS, Alan. The Velvet Rage. Da Capo Press, 2012 (originally published 2005).

DUFF, Charles, Charley's Woods. Zuleika, 2017.

FRENCH-BEYTAGH, Gonville. Encountering Darkness. Collins, 1973.

FRANKL, Viktor, E. Man's Search for Meaning. Ebury Publishing, 2004.

FROMM, Erich. To Have or To Be. Bloomsbury Academic, 2013 (originally published 1976).

HARRIS, Russ (Dr.). The Happiness Trap. Exisle Publishing, 2007.

HAYES, Bill. Insomnia City. Bloomsbury USA, 2017.

JOHNSON, Malcolm. Diary of a Gay Priest. Christian Alternative, 2013.

KEMPIS à Thomas. The Imitation of Christ. Penquin Classic 2013.

KIRK, Kenneth. The Vision of God. James Clarke, 1990 (originally published 1931).

LEMON, Don. Transparent. Farrah Gray Publishing, 2011.

LEWIS, C.S. The Four Loves. HarperCollins, 2002 (originally published 1960).

LEWIS, C.S. Mere Christianity. HarperCollins, 2011 (originally published 1952).

LEWIS, C.S. The Screwtape Letters. William Collins, 2016 (originally published 1942).

LEWIS, C.S. Surprised by Joy. William Collins, 2016 (originally published 1952).

LINGS, K. Renato. Love Lost in Translation: Homosexuality and the Bible. Trafford 2013.

MacCULLOCH, Diarmaid. A History of the Church. Allen Lane for Penquin Books, 2009. Also, his BBC 2 Series Sex and the Church, April 2015.

OZANNE, Jayne. Only Love. Darton, Longman & Todd, 2018.

REED, Bruce. The Dynamics of Religion. Darton, Longman & Todd, 1978.

SEWELL, Brian. Outcast. Quartet, 2011.

SACKS, Oliver. On the Move: A Life. Picador 2015.

SANGSTER W. E. Teach us to Pray. Epworth Press 1951.

WEATHERHEAD, Leslie. Prescription for Anxiety. Hodder & Stoughton (1956).

WEATHERHEAD, Leslie. Psychology, Religion and Healing.

Stewart Press, 2007. (originally published 1951).

WEATHERHEAD, Leslie. The Transforming Friendship. Abingdon Classics, 1990. (originally published 1929).

WHARTON, James. Out in the Army: My Life as a Gay Soldier. Biteback Publishing, 2013.

WILDEBLOOD, Peter. Against the Law. Weidenfeld & Nicolson, 1999.

WILLIAMS, Harry. The True Wilderness. Continuum International, 2002. (originally published 1965).

WILLIAMS BIANCO, Margery. The Velveteen Rabbit. Board Edition 2007.

WILSON, Alan. More Perfect Union? Darton, Longman & Todd, 2014.

Appendix

Copy of my letter sent to Jayne Ozanne, the Representative for the Diocese of Oxford who was attending the Synod of the Church of England in July 2017.

Dear Jayne,

I have read in the Church Times dated 30th June 2017 that the General Synod is being urged to condemn conversion therapy as 'unethical and harmful'. I am now ninety years old and a Priest in the Church of England living in retirement at Charterhouse, London. I am a celibate homosexual and have suffered a lifetime of reactive depression resulting from my inability to accept my sexual orientation. Like yourself, I was brought up as an Evangelical Christian. The trouble started for real when in my early twenties a Fundamentalist Christian sought to exorcise my 'demon' as he called it but failed to do so. This resulted in a breakdown and hospitalisation where I was administered Electric Current Therapy. After that, I had testosterone injections for a year administered by my local GP. Then followed a course of Freudian psychotherapy in the hope that my sexual orientation would be redirected. I was then given lithium at St. Thomas's Hospital followed by no end of personal counselling, therapy and prayer, all of which totally failed to make any difference to my sexual inclinations. I once contemplated Aversion Therapy but the knowledge of what is done to the patient revolted me. On two occasions, I have contemplated suicide.

My misery did not end there; for most of my life I have acted as a straight man but despite that I have suffered people's homophobia in many forms both from people who have no faith (who are simply prejudiced out of ignorance) as well as Christians who sadly treat the scriptures in a literalistic sense, ignoring that it is prescientific; using it without regard to its original purpose or context and refusing to consider contemporary developments in our understanding of human nature thus bringing the Church into disrepute.

I hope with all my heart that your private member's motion asking the Synod 'that such treatment is unethical and harmful' as it does not work, will be accepted.

May God support you in all your endeavors to bring about an end once and for all to the Churches' homophobia in all its forms which throughout the ages has caused so much misery and suffering to countless thousands of people who were made in the image of God.

You may use this information as you think fit. I have for the last three years been writing my autobiography and now it is being edited with a view to publication.

With prayer and good wishes,

S. R underhir

The Rev. Stanley Underhill

Printed in Great Britain
by Amazon